Project Management Institute

PRACTICE STANDARD FOR PROJECT RISK MANAGEMENT

ISBN: 978-1-933890-38-8

Published by:
Project Management Institute, Inc.
14 Campus Boulevard
Newtown Square, Pennsylvania 19073-3299 USA.
Phone: +1-610-356-4600
Fax: +1-610-356-4647
E-mail: customercare@pmi.org

Internet: www.pmi.org

PMI Publications welcomes corrections and comments on its books. Please feel free to send comments on typographical, formatting, or other errors. Simply make a copy of the relevant page of the book, mark the error, and send it to: Book Editor, PMI Publications, 14 Campus Boulevard, Newtown Square, PA 19073-3299 USA.

To inquire about discounts for resale or educational purposes, please contact the PMI Book Service Center.
PMI Book Service Center
P.O. Box 932683, Atlanta, GA 31193-2683 USA
Phone: 1-866-276-4764 (within the U.S. or Canada) or +1-770-280-4129 (globally)
Fax: +1-770-280-4113
E-mail: book.orders@pmi.org

The paper used in this book complies with the Permanent Paper Standard issued by the National Information Standards Organization (Z39.48—1984).

10 9 8 7 6 5 4

NOTICE

The Project Management Institute, Inc. (PMI) standards and guideline publications, of which the document contained herein is one, are developed through a voluntary consensus standards development process. This process brings together volunteers and/or seeks out the views of persons who have an interest in the topic covered by this publication. While PMI administers the process and establishes rules to promote fairness in the development of consensus, it does not write the document and it does not independently test, evaluate, or verify the accuracy or completeness of any information or the soundness of any judgments contained in its standards and guideline publications.

PMI disclaims liability for any personal injury, property or other damages of any nature whatsoever, whether special, indirect, consequential or compensatory, directly or indirectly resulting from the publication, use of application, or reliance on this document. PMI disclaims and makes no guaranty or warranty, expressed or implied, as to the accuracy or completeness of any information published herein, and disclaims and makes no warranty that the information in this document will fulfill any of your particular purposes or needs. PMI does not undertake to guarantee the performance of any individual manufacturer or seller's products or services by virtue of this standard or guide.

In publishing and making this document available, PMI is not undertaking to render professional or other services for or on behalf of any person or entity, nor is PMI undertaking to perform any duty owed by any person or entity to someone else. Anyone using this document should rely on his or her own independent judgment or, as appropriate, seek the advice of a competent professional in determining the exercise of reasonable care in any given circumstances. Information and other standards on the topic covered by this publication may be available from other sources, which the user may wish to consult for additional views or information not covered by this publication.

PMI has no power, nor does it undertake to police or enforce compliance with the contents of this document. PMI does not certify, test, or inspect products, designs, or installations for safety or health purposes. Any certification or other statement of compliance with any health or safety-related information in this document shall not be attributable to PMI and is solely the responsibility of the certifier or maker of the statement.

TABLE OF CONTENTS

LIST OF FIGURES

CHAPTER 1

INTRODUCTION

Project Management Institute (PMI) practice standards are guides to the use of a tool, technique, or process identified in *A Guide to the Project Management Body of Knowledge* (*PMBOK® Guide* – Fourth Edition) or other PMI standards. Practice standards are targeted at audiences who participate in the management of projects. This includes project managers, project personnel, contract personnel, supervisors, and other project stakeholders.

A PMI practice standard describes processes, activities, inputs, and outputs for a specific Knowledge Area. It provides information on what the significant process, tool, or technique is, what it does, why it is significant, when it should be performed or executed, and, if necessary for further clarification, who should perform the process. A practice standard does not prescribe how the process is to be implemented, leaving that subject for other forums such as handbooks, manuals, and courses.

This chapter includes the following sections:

1.1 Purpose of the Practice Standard for Project Risk Management

1.2 Project Risk Management Definition

1.3 Role of Project Risk Management in Project Management

1.4 Good Risk Management Practice

1.5 Critical Success Factors for Project Risk Management

1.1 Purpose of the *Practice Standard for Project Risk Management*

The purpose of the *Practice Standard for Project Risk Management* is to (*a*) provide a standard for project management practitioners and other stakeholders that defines the aspects of Project Risk Management that are recognized as good practice on most projects most of the time and (*b*) provide a standard that is globally applicable and consistently applied. This practice standard has a descriptive purpose rather than one used for training or educational purposes.

The *Practice Standard for Project Risk Management* covers risk management as it is applied to single projects only. Like the *PMBOK® Guide* – Fourth Edition, this practice standard does not cover risk in programs or portfolios of projects.

Chapter 11 of the *PMBOK® Guide* – Fourth Edition, is the basis for the *Practice Standard for Project Risk Management*. This practice standard is consistent with that chapter, emphasizing the concepts and principles relating to Project Risk Management. It is aligned with other PMI practice standards.

Figure 1-1 compares the purposes of this practice standard to those of the *PMBOK® Guide* – Fourth Edition and textbooks, handbooks, and courses.

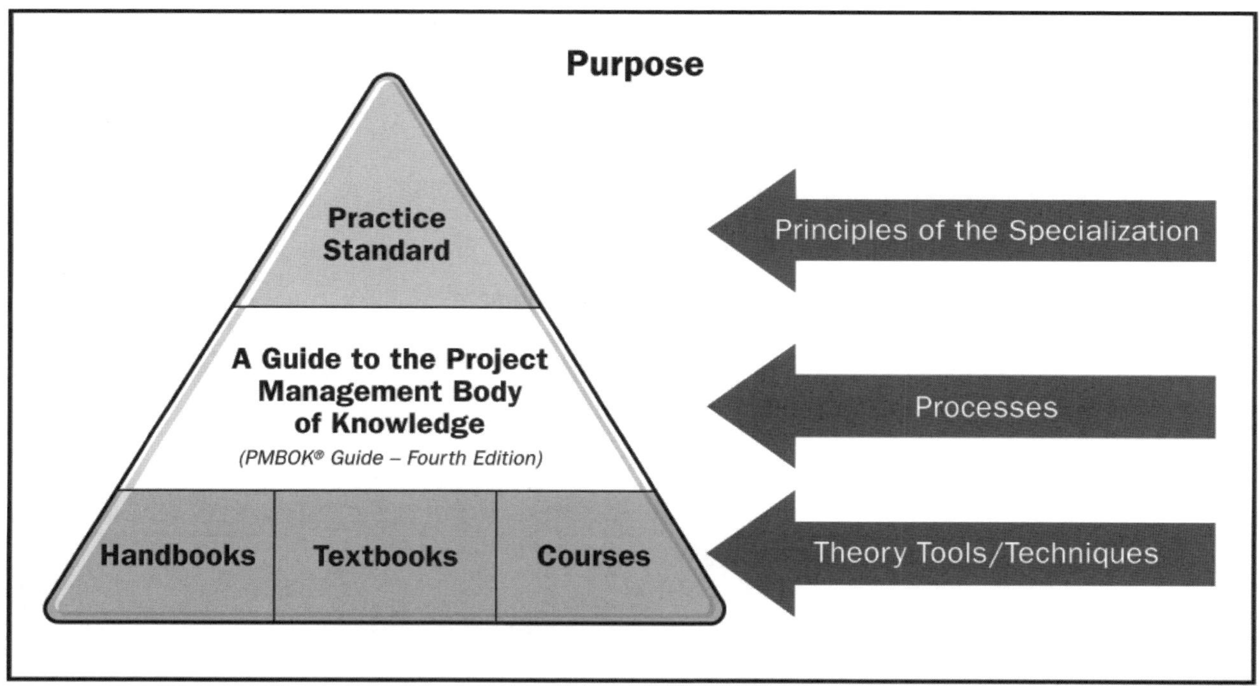

Figure 1-1. Hierarchy of PMI Project Risk Management Resources

This practice standard is organized in three main sections:

1. Introductory material including the framework, purpose, principles, context of, and introduction to Project Risk Management processes as defined in the *PMBOK® Guide* – Fourth Edition.
2. Principles underlying the six Project Risk Management processes in the *PMBOK® Guide* – Fourth Edition. The six processes are as follows:
   - Plan Risk Management,
   - Identify Risks,
   - Perform Qualitative Risk Analysis,
   - Perform Quantitative Risk Analysis,
   - Plan Risk Responses, and
   - Monitor and Control Risks.

   Each of these six processes is described in a chapter that addresses the following four topics: (*a*) purpose and objectives of the process; (*b*) critical success factors for the process; (*c*) tools and techniques for the process; and (*d*) documenting the results of the process.
3. A glossary of terms which are used in this practice standard.

This practice standard emphasizes those principles that are fundamental to effective, comprehensive, and successful Project Risk Management. These principles can and should be stated at a general level for several reasons:

1. Principles are expected to be agreed upon now and to be valid in the future. While tools and techniques are constantly evolving, the principles have more stability and persistence.
2. Different projects, organizations, and situations will require different approaches to Project Risk Management. In particular, risk management is a discipline that contains a series of processes to apply to both large and small projects. Risk management will be more effective if its practice is tailored to the project and congruent with the organizational culture, processes and assets. There are many different ways of conducting risk management that may comply with the principles of Project Risk Management as presented in this practice standard.
3. The principles are applicable to projects carried out in a global context, reflecting the many business and organizational arrangements between participants, for example, joint ventures between commercial and national companies, government and non-government organizations, and the cross-cultural environment often found on these project teams.

The principles described herein can be used as a check for an organization's processes. Practitioners can establish processes specific to their particular situation, project, or organization and then compare them with these principles, thus validating them against good Project Risk Management practice.

1.2 Project Risk Management Definition

The definition of Project Risk Management, as defined in the *PMBOK® Guide* – Fourth Edition, is the basis for this practice standard: "Project Risk Management includes the processes concerned with conducting risk management planning, identification, analysis, responses, and monitoring and control on a project." The *PMBOK® Guide* – Fourth Edition also states: "The objectives of Project Risk Management are to increase the probability and impact of positive events, and decrease the probability and impact of negative events in the project." In the *PMBOK® Guide* – Fourth Edition, "project risk is an uncertain event or condition that, if it occurs, has a positive or negative effect on a project's objectives." Project objectives include scope, schedule, cost, and quality.

Project Risk Management aims to identify and prioritize risks in advance of their occurrence, and provide action-oriented information to project managers. This orientation requires consideration of events that may or may not occur and are therefore described in terms of likelihood or probability of occurrence in addition to other dimensions such as their impact on objectives.

1.3 Role of Project Risk Management in Project Management

Project Risk Management is not an optional activity: it is essential to successful project management. It should be applied to all projects and hence be included in project plans and operational documents. In this way, it becomes an integral part of every aspect of managing the project, in every phase and in every process group.

Many of the project management processes address planning the project, from concept to final design and from procurement through daily management of execution and close-out. These processes often assume an unrealistic degree of certainty about the project and, therefore, they need to include treatment of project risks.

Project Risk Management addresses the uncertainty in project estimates and assumptions. Therefore, it builds upon and extends other project management processes. For instance, project scheduling provides dates and critical paths based on activity durations and resource availability assumed to be known with certainty. Quantitative risk analysis explores the uncertainty in the estimated durations and may provide alternative dates and critical paths that are more realistic given the risks to the project.

Project Risk Management is not a substitute for the other project management processes. On the contrary, Project Risk Management requires that these project management processes (e.g. scheduling, budgeting, and change management) be performed at the level of the best practices available. Project Risk Management adds the perspective of project risk to the outputs of those other processes and adds to their value by taking risk into account. For instance, risk management provides the basis upon which to estimate the amount of cost and schedule contingency reserves that are needed to cover risk response actions to a required level of confidence for meeting project objectives.

There is a paradox about project risk that affects most projects. In the early stages of a project, the level of risk exposure is at its maximum but information on the project risks is at a minimum. This situation does not mean that a project should not go forward because little is known at that time. Rather, there may be different ways of approaching the project that have different risk implications. The more this situation is recognized, the more realistic the project plans and expectations of results will be.

A risk management approach is applicable throughout a project's life cycle. The earlier in the project life cycle that the risks are recognized, the more realistic the project plans and expectations of results will be. Risk management continues to add value as project planning progresses and more information becomes available about all aspects and components of the project and its environment, such as stakeholders, scope, time, and cost, as well as the corresponding assumptions and constraints. The balance between project flexibility and knowledge about project risk needs to be reviewed regularly and optimized as the plans develop.

It is true that as the project plan becomes set with fundamental decisions, agreements, and contracts in place, the options for making substantial changes to capture opportunities or mitigate threats are reduced. During project execution, risk management processes monitor the changes the project undergoes for new risks that may emerge so that appropriate responses to them can be developed, as well as check for existing risks that are no longer plausible. Project Risk Management plays a role in providing realistic expectations for the completion dates and cost of the project even if there are few options for changing the future.

Finally, throughout the project and during project closure, risk-related lessons are reviewed in order to contribute to organizational learning and support continuous improvement of Project Risk Management practice.

1.4 Good Risk Management Practice

Project Risk Management is a valuable component of project management and it enhances the value of the other project management processes. As with all of these processes, Project Risk Management should be conducted in a manner consistent with existing organizational practices and policies. In addition, like the other processes involved in project management, Project Risk Management should be conducted in a way that is appropriate to the project. Project Risk Management should recognize the business challenges as well as the multi-cultural environment associated with an increasingly global environment including many joint venture projects and customers, suppliers, and workforces spread around the globe.

Changes in the project management plan that result from the Project Risk Management process may require decisions at the appropriate level of management to reassign personnel, establish or modify budgets, make commitments to others outside the project, interact with regulators, and comply with the rules of accounting and law. Project Risk Management should be conducted in compliance with these internal and external requirements.

Project Risk Management should always be conducted on an ethical basis, in keeping with the Project Management code of ethics or conduct. Honesty, responsibility, realism, professionalism and fair dealing with others are among the characteristics of successful Project Risk Management. Effective Project Risk Management benefits from robust communication and consultation with stakeholders. This enables agreement among stakeholders that Project Risk Management in general, and risk identification, analysis, and response, in particular, should be carried out in a realistic and objective way and should not be subject to political or other unreasonable influences.

Project Risk Management should be conducted on all projects. The degree, level of detail, sophistication of tools, and amount of time and resources applied to Project Risk Management should be in proportion to the characteristics of the project under management and the value that they can add to the outcome. Thus, a large project that provides value to an important customer would theoretically require more resources, time, and attention to Project Risk Management than would a smaller, short-term, internal project that can be conducted in the background with a flexible deadline.

Each of the Project Risk Management processes should be scaled to be appropriate to the project under management during the Plan Risk Management process and reviewed periodically to determine if the decisions made in that process remain appropriate.

1.5 Critical Success Factors for Project Risk Management

Figure 1-2. Critical Success Factors for Project Risk Management

Specific criteria for success of each Project Risk Management process are listed in the chapters dealing with those processes. The general criteria for success include:

- *Recognize the Value of Risk Management*—Project Risk Management should be recognized as a valuable discipline that provides a positive potential return on investment for organizational management, project stakeholders (both internal and external), project management, and team members.
- *Individual Commitment/Responsibility*—Project participants and stakeholders should all accept responsibility for undertaking risk-related activities as required. Risk management is everybody's responsibility.
- *Open and Honest Communication*—Everyone should be involved in the Project Risk Management process. Any actions or attitudes that hinder communication about project risk reduce the effectiveness of Project Risk Management in terms of proactive approaches and effective decision-making.
- *Organizational Commitment*—Organizational commitment can only be established if risk management is aligned with the organization's goals and values. Project Risk Management may require a higher level of managerial support than other project management disciplines because handling some of the risks will require approval of or responses from others at levels above the project manager.
- *Risk Effort Scaled to Project*—Project Risk Management activities should be consistent with the value of the project to the organization and with its level of project risk, its scale, and other organizational constraints. In particular, the cost of Project Risk Management should be appropriate to its potential value to the project and the organization.
- *Integration with Project Management*—Project Risk Management does not exist in a vacuum, isolated from other project management processes. Successful Project Risk Management requires the correct execution of the other project management processes.

These critical success factors for Project Risk Management are illustrated in Figure 1-2.

1.6 Conclusion

The principles of Project Risk Management described in this practice standard should be appropriately applied based on the specifics of a project and the organizational environment. Project Risk Management provides benefits when it is implemented according to good practice principles and with organizational commitment to taking the decisions and performing actions in an open and unbiased manner.

CHAPTER 2

PRINCIPLES AND CONCEPTS

2.1 Introduction

This chapter introduces the key ideas required to understand and apply Project Risk Management to projects following the approach described in Chapter 11 of the *PMBOK® Guide* – Fourth Edition. These principles and concepts are generally consistent with other approaches to Project Risk Management commonly used although the terminology may differ in some details.

The execution of the Project Risk Management process is dealt with in subsequent chapters of this practice standard and so is not discussed here.

2.2 Definition of Project Risk

The word "risk" is used in many ways in everyday language and in various specialist disciplines. Its use in the *PMBOK® Guide* – Fourth Edition is consistent with other risk management standards and process descriptions. The definition of project risk given in the *PMBOK® Guide* – Fourth Edition is as follows:

> Project risk is an uncertain event or condition that, if it occurs, has a positive or a negative effect on a project's objectives.

This definition includes two key dimensions of risk: uncertainty and effect on a project's objectives. When assessing the importance of a project risk, these two dimensions must both be considered. The uncertainty dimension may be described using the term "probability" and the effect may be called "impact" (though other descriptors are possible, such as "likelihood" and "consequence").

The definition of risk includes both distinct events which are uncertain but can be clearly described, and more general conditions which are less specific but also may give risk to uncertainty. The definition of project risk also encompasses uncertain events which could have a negative effect on a project's objectives, as well as those which could have a positive effect. These two types of risk are called, respectively, threats and opportunities. It is important to address both threats and opportunities within a unified Project Risk Management process. This allows for the gain of synergies and efficiencies such as addressing both in the same analyses and coordinating the responses to both if they overlap or can reinforce each other.

Risks are uncertain future events or conditions which may or may not occur, but which would matter if they did occur. It is important to distinguish risks from risk-related features, such as cause and effect. Causes are events or circumstances which currently exist or are certain to exist in the future and which might give rise to risks. Effects are conditional future events or conditions which would directly affect one or more project objectives if the associated risk occurs. The cause-risk-effect chain can be used in a structured risk statement or risk description to ensure that each of these three elements is properly described (see Section 5.3).

When a risk event occurs, it ceases to become uncertain. Threats which occur may be called issues or problems; opportunities which occur may be called benefits. Both issues/problems and benefits entail project management actions that are outside the scope of the Project Risk Management process.

2.3 Individual Risks and Overall Project Risk

It is useful to consider project risk at two levels: individual risks and overall project risk.

Individual risks are specific events or conditions that might affect project objectives. An individual risk may positively or negatively affect one or more of the project objectives, elements, or tasks. Understanding individual risks can assist in determining how to apply effort and resources to enhance the chances of project success. Day-to-day Project Risk Management focuses on these individual risks in order to enhance the prospects of a successful project outcome.

Overall project risk represents the effect of uncertainty on the project as a whole. Overall project risk is more than the sum of individual risks on a project, since it applies to the whole project rather than to individual elements or tasks. It represents the exposure of stakeholders to the implications of variations in project outcome. It is an important component of strategic decision-making, program and portfolio management, and project governance where investments are sanctioned or cancelled and priorities are set. At these higher levels, it is necessary to set realistic targets for the cost and duration of a project, establish the contingency reserve levels required to protect the project stakeholders, set appropriate project priorities, and judge whether the risk of overall success is increasing or decreasing as implementation advances.

2.4 Stakeholder Risk Attitudes

The risk attitudes of the project stakeholders determine the extent to which an individual risk or overall project risk matters. A wide range of factors influence risk attitude. These include the scale of the project within the range of stakeholders' overall activities, the strength of public commitments made about the performance of the project, and the stakeholders' sensitivity to issues such as environmental impacts, industrial relations, and other factors. Stakeholder risk attitudes usually result in a desire for increased certainty in project outcomes, and may express a preference for one project objective over another. How risk is regarded is usually also strongly influenced by an organization's culture. Different organizations are more or less open, and this often impacts the way risk management can be applied.

Understanding stakeholders' attitudes toward risk is an important component of risk management planning that precedes risk identification and analysis, in order to optimize both project success and stakeholder satisfaction with the project's results. These attitudes should be identified and managed proactively and deliberately throughout the Project Risk Management process. They may differ from one project to another for the same stakeholders and will usually differ from one group of stakeholders to another. In fact a single stakeholder may adopt different risk attitudes at various stages in the same project.

It is also important to understand the particular implications of stakeholder risk attitudes on projects where the team is international, cross-industry, or multi-organizational.

2.5 Iterative Process

It is the nature of projects that circumstances change as they are being planned and executed. The amount of information available about risks will usually increase as time goes on. Some risks will occur while others will not, new risks will arise or be discovered, and the characteristics of those already identified may change. As a result, the Project Risk Management processes should be repeated and the corresponding plans progressively elaborated throughout the lifetime of the project.

To ensure that Project Risk Management remains effective, the identification and analysis of risks should be revisited periodically, the progress on risk response actions should be monitored, and the action plans adjusted accordingly. If external circumstances change significantly, it may also be necessary to revisit the risk management planning process.

The development of an initial risk management plan and risk assessment is the start of the process, not the end. The frequency and depth of reviews and updates will depend on the nature of the project, the volatility of the environment in which the project is being implemented, and the timing of other project management reviews and updates.

2.6 Communication

Project Risk Management cannot take place in isolation. Success relies heavily on communication throughout the process.

Risk identification and analysis depend on comprehensive input from stakeholders in a project to ensure that nothing significant is overlooked and that risks are realistically assessed. The credibility of the process and the commitment of those who should act to manage risks can be assured only if the way the process operates and the conclusions it produces are understood and seen as credible by all concerned. This demands effective and honest communication from the Project Risk Management process to the rest of the project team and other project stakeholders. Communication of the results of the Project Risk Management process should be targeted to meet the specific needs of each stakeholder and should be reflected within the overall project communications strategy with each stakeholder's responsibility and role in risk management identified and agreed-upon.

2.7 Responsibility for Project Risk Management

It may be considered simplistic to say "risk management is everyone's responsibility" as previously stated. However it is important that management of project risk is not left to a few risk specialists. Project Risk Management should be included as an integral part of all other project processes. Since project risks can affect project objectives, anyone with an interest in achieving those objectives should play a role in Project Risk Management. The specific roles depend on the project team members' and other stakeholders' place within the project and their relation to project objectives. Roles and responsibilities for Project Risk Management should be clearly defined and communicated, and individuals should be held responsible and accountable for results. This includes allocating responsibility for specific activities within the risk process, as well as for resulting actions required to implement agreed-upon responses. Responsibility should also be allocated for ensuring that risk-related lessons are captured for future use.

2.8 Project Manager's Role for Project Risk Management

The project manager has particular responsibilities in relation to the Project Risk Management process. The project manager has overall responsibility for delivering a successful project which fully meets the defined objectives. The project manager is accountable for the day-to-day management of the project, including effective risk management. The role of the project manager may include:

- Encouraging senior management support for Project Risk Management activities.
- Determining the acceptable levels of risk for the project in consultation with stakeholders.
- Developing and approving the risk management plan.
- Promoting the Project Risk Management process for the project.
- Facilitating open and honest communication about risk within the project team and with management and other stakeholders.
- Participating in all aspects of the Project Risk Management process.
- Approving risk responses and associated actions prior to implementation.
- Applying project contingency funds to deal with identified risks that occur during the project.
- Overseeing risk management by subcontractors and suppliers.
- Regularly reporting risk status to key stakeholders, with recommendations for appropriate strategic decisions and actions to maintain acceptable risk exposure.
- Escalating identified risks to senior management where appropriate: such risks include any which are outside the authority or control of the project manager, any which require input or action from outside the project, and any for which the release of management reserve funds might be appropriate.
- Monitoring the efficiency and effectiveness of the Project Risk Management process.
- Auditing risk responses for their effectiveness and documenting lessons learned.

CHAPTER 3

INTRODUCTION TO PROJECT RISK MANAGEMENT PROCESSES

3.1 Project Risk Management and Project Management

All projects are uncertain. Uncertainty is inevitable since projects are unique and temporary undertakings based on assumptions and constraints, delivering project results to multiple stakeholders with different requirements. Project management can be seen as an attempt to control this uncertain environment, through the use of structured and disciplined techniques such as estimating, planning, cost control, task allocation, earned value analysis, monitoring and review meetings, etc. Each of these elements of project management has a role in defining or controlling the uncertainty which is inherent in all projects.

Project Risk Management provides an approach by which uncertainty can be understood, assessed, and managed within projects. As such it forms an integral part of project management, and effective Project Risk Management is a critical success factor for project success.

For project management to be fully effective, however, it is important that Project Risk Management is not viewed as an optional process or performed as an additional overhead task. Since many elements of project management address inherent uncertainty, the interface between structured Project Risk Management and the other processes of project management needs to be clear. The outputs of Project Risk Management should be taken into account within many of the project management processes. They can, for example, impact:

- Estimating resource requirements, cost, or duration;
- Assessing the impact of proposed scope changes;
- Planning or re-planning the forward strategy of the project;
- Allocating resources to tasks; and
- Reporting progress to stakeholders.

None of these actions can be performed properly without a clear view of the risk involved, as determined during the Project Risk Management process. In other words, project management process effectiveness is increased by using the information and results from Project Risk Management.

In addition, effective Project Risk Management requires input from other project management processes. Outputs such as the work breakdown structure (WBS), estimates, the project schedule, assumptions list, etc. are all important prerequisites for effective Project Risk Management.

3.2 Project Risk Management Processes

The defined steps of Project Risk Management describe a structured approach for understanding and managing risk on a project. This chapter outlines the steps required for effective Project Risk Management. Each step is described in more detail in subsequent chapters.

As previously defined, project risk is an uncertain event or condition that, if it occurs, has a positive or negative effect on a project's objectives. From this definition, it is clear that risks only exist in relation to objectives. It is therefore essential at the start of the Project Risk Management process to clearly define the objectives. It is also clear that different projects are exposed to different levels of risk, so each step in the Project Risk Management process should be scalable to meet the varying degrees of risk. Scalable elements of the process include:

- Available resources,
- Methodology and processes used,
- Tools and techniques used,
- Supporting infrastructure,
- Review and update frequency, and
- Reporting requirements.

As a precondition for a successful Project Risk Management implementation, it is important to have a clear understanding of the risk thresholds that define the key stakeholders' views on acceptable levels of risk, as well as a framework against which identified risks can be assessed.

As a result, the Project Risk Management process always starts with an initiation step. This is required in order to ensure a common understanding and agreement of the team and other stakeholders on the approach and parameters that will be applied in managing risk in this project, as well as the scope and objectives of the Project Risk Management process itself. Project Risk Management activities, resources, and attention should be appropriate to the project since different projects warrant different levels of risk management application. The main actions to provide the required tailoring are as follows:

- Define those objectives against which risks will be identified,
- Define how the elements of the Project Risk Management process will be scaled for this project, and
- Define risk thresholds, tolerances, and the assessment framework.

The outputs from this initial step should be documented, communicated, and then reviewed by the stakeholders to ensure a common understanding of the scope and objectives for the Project Risk Management process. The document should be formally approved at a senior level.

Once the Project Risk Management scope and objectives are agreed upon, it is possible to start identifying risks, being careful to distinguish genuine risks from non-risks (such as causes, effects, problems, issues etc.). A variety of risk identification techniques is available, each with its own strengths and weaknesses. One or more techniques should be selected as appropriate for meeting the needs of the specific project. The aim is to expose and document all knowable risks, recognizing that some risks will be inherently unknowable and others will emerge later in the project. The emergent nature of risk requires the Project Risk Management process to be iterative, repeating the Identify Risks process in order to find risks which were not evident earlier in the project. Input should be sought from a wide range of project stakeholders when identifying risks, since each will have a different perspective on the risks facing the project. Historical records and project documents should also be reviewed to identify risks for this project.

All identified risks are recorded. Ideally, a risk owner is designated for each identified risk. It is the responsibility of the risk owner to manage the corresponding risk through all of the subsequent Project Risk Management processes.

Following risk identification, it is necessary to evaluate the importance of each risk, in order to prioritize individual risks for further attention, evaluate the level of overall project risk, and determine appropriate responses. Risk evaluation can be performed using qualitative techniques to address individual risks, using quantitative techniques to consider the overall effect of risk on the project outcome, or using both in combination. These two approaches require different types of data, but where both qualitative and quantitative techniques are used, an integrated approach should be adopted.

Qualitative techniques are used to gain a better understanding of individual risks, considering a range of characteristics such as probability of occurrence, degree of impact on project objectives, manageability, timing of possible impacts, relationships with other risks, common causes or effects, etc. Understanding and prioritizing risks is an essential prerequisite to managing them, so qualitative techniques are used on most projects. The outputs from qualitative assessments should be documented and communicated to key project stakeholders and form a basis for determining appropriate responses.

Quantitative techniques provide insights into the combined effect of identified risks on the project outcome. These techniques take into account probabilistic or project-wide effects, such as correlation between risks, interdependency, and feedback loops, thereby indicating the degree of overall risk faced by the project. The result is an indication of the degree of overall risk faced by the project. The results of quantitative analysis should be used to focus the development of appropriate responses, particularly the calculation of required contingency reserve levels, and must be documented and communicated to inform subsequent actions. Quantitative techniques may not be required for all projects to ensure effective management of risk.

Once individual risks have been prioritized and the degree of overall project risk exposure is understood, appropriate risk responses should be developed using an iterative process which continues until an optimal set of responses has been developed. A range of possible response strategies exists for both threats and opportunities. The risk owner should select a suitable strategy for each individual risk, based on its characteristics and assessed priority, ensuring that the strategy is achievable, affordable, cost effective, and appropriate. The use of a single strategy that addresses several related risks should be considered whenever possible. The risk owner is responsible for defining actions to implement the chosen strategy. These actions may be delegated to action owners as appropriate. The risk owner should monitor actions to determine their effectiveness, and also to identify any secondary risks which may arise because of the implementation of risk responses. In addition to individual risk responses, actions may be taken to respond to overall project risk. All response strategies and actions should be documented and communicated to key project stakeholders and incorporated into the project plan.

It is essential that agreed-upon actions are implemented; otherwise the risk exposure of the project remains unchanged. It is also vital that the Project Risk Management process be repeated at regular intervals throughout the life of the project. This will enable the project team to reevaluate the status of previously identified risks, to identify emergent and secondary risks, and to determine the effectiveness of the Project Risk Management process.

The steps outlined previously form the Project Risk Management process. These are detailed in subsequent chapters, as follows:

- **Plan Risk Management (Chapter 4)**—Defines the scope and objectives of the Project Risk Management process, and ensures that the risk process is fully integrated into wider project management.
- **Identify Risks (Chapter 5)**—Identifies as many knowable risks as practicable.
- **Perform Qualitative Risk Analysis (Chapter 6)**—Evaluates key characteristics of individual risks enabling them to be prioritized for further action.
- **Perform Quantitative Risk Analysis (Chapter 7)**—Evaluates the combined effect of risks on the overall project outcome.
- **Plan Risk Responses (Chapter 8)**—Determines appropriate response strategies and actions for each individual risk and for overall project risk, and integrates them into a consolidated project management plan.
- **Monitor and Control Risks (Chapter 9)**—Implements agreed-upon actions, reviews changes in project risk exposure, identifies additional risk management actions as required, and assesses the effectiveness of the Project Risk Management process.

Figure 3-1 shows the flow of control and information between the various steps within the Project Risk Management process.

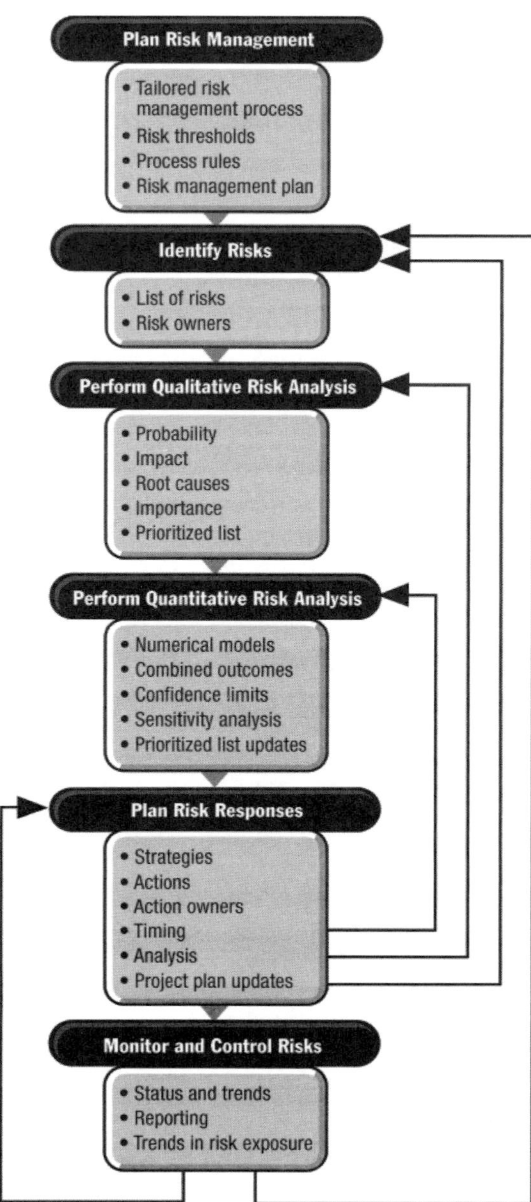

Figure 3-1. Project Risk Management Process Flow Diagram

CHAPTER 4

PLAN RISK MANAGEMENT

4.1 Purpose and Objectives of the Plan Risk Management Process

The objectives of the Plan Risk Management process are to develop the overall risk management strategy for the project, to decide how the risk management processes will be executed, and to integrate Project Risk Management with all other project management activities.

Effective risk management requires creation of a risk management plan. This plan describes how the risk management processes should be carried out and how they fit in with the other project management processes. On a broader level, it describes the relationships among Project Risk Management, general project management, and the management processes in the rest of the organization. To provide the greatest benefit, initial risk management planning should be carried out early in the overall planning of the project, and the corresponding risk management activities integrated into the overall project management plan. The risk management plan may subsequently need to be adapted as the needs of the project and its stakeholders become clearer or change.

Although the Project Risk Management processes form an integral part of the overall project management plan, a budget in terms of resources, cost, and time for the specific risk management activities should be established in order to better track, control, and, as necessary, defend the corresponding expenditures throughout the project. The cost of treating the risks themselves should be included appropriately in the project budget, while the risk management plan should describe how this part of the project budget is evaluated, allocated, and managed. The risk management plan will define the monitoring methods to ensure that the corresponding expenditures are tracked appropriately, as well as the conditions under which the approved budget for risk management can be modified.

In the same way that project management is a process of progressive elaboration, risk management activities need to be repeated throughout the project. The risk management plan should define both the normal frequency for repeating the processes as well as specific or exceptional conditions under which the corresponding actions should be initiated. The corresponding risk management activities should be integrated into the project management plan.

There are two categories of success criteria for risk management: those for success of the project in general, and those for success of Project Risk Management.

- **Project-Related Criteria.** To assess the success of Project Risk Management, the stakeholders must agree on an acceptable level of results for the project-related criteria (such as cost, time, and scope). In order to ensure consistency and agreement among stakeholders, the risk management plan should present these objectives with reference to the project definition documents. To provide guidance in risk management, particularly in prioritizing risk responses, stakeholders should also prioritize each project objective.
- **Process-Related Criteria.** The measures for success in Project Risk Management depend on a number of factors, such as the inherent level of uncertainty of the project. For example, the Project Risk Management process for a research project needs to address more unforeseen changes than for a project with a more predictable environment. A research Project Risk Management process may be considered a success even if it results in more variance from the baseline than would be allowable for a successful process in a more predictable project.

The level of risk that is considered acceptable in a project depends on the risk attitudes of the relevant stakeholders. The risk attitudes of both the organization and the stakeholders may be influenced by a number of factors, all of which need to be identified. These include their inherent tolerance for uncertainty, and the relative importance to them of achieving or missing specific project objectives. The output of this analysis should then be taken into account for setting thresholds and providing weighting factors when applying the Project Risk Management processes in the specific project.

Guidelines and rules for escalating risk-related information to management and other stakeholders should reflect the risk attitudes and expectations of the corresponding stakeholders. The project manager should maintain effective communication with the stakeholders as the project evolves, in order to become aware of any changes in the stakeholders' attitudes and adapt the risk management approach to take any new facts into account.

It is important that the participants share a common understanding of all terms used to describe the risks, and that the critical values and thresholds that will serve as parameters for the tools should be defined in a manner consistent with the scope of the project and the attitudes of the stakeholders. If qualitative analysis uses such terms as "high impact" or "medium probability," these should be defined objectively in the risk management plan. Similarly, the risk management plan should specify any key numerical values required in quantitative analysis or for decision-making in risk response planning or risk monitoring and control.

Risk management planning should establish the type and level of risk detail to be addressed and provide a template of the risk register that will be used for recording risk-related information. The risk management plan should also indicate the intensity of effort and the frequency with which the various Project Risk Management processes should be applied; this depends on the characteristics of the project as well as on the specified risk management objectives.

In order for the Project Risk Management processes to be carried out correctly and effectively, the project team and other stakeholders need to know where and when they will be expected to participate, their criteria for determining success, their level of authority, and what action to take relative to actions or decisions beyond this level. The risk management plan specifies the project's risk management roles and responsibilities and defines the corresponding expectations for both senior management and project personnel.

Risk-related communication occurs at two levels: (a) within the project team, and (b) between the project team and the other project stakeholders. The principles for each of these categories of communication are defined in the risk management plan. For the team, the plan describes the frequency and scope of the various risk management meetings and reports required to carry out the corresponding Project Risk Management processes as well as the structure and content of such meetings and reports. For the other stakeholders, the plan sets their expectations as to the structure, content, and frequency of routine documents to be received as well as the way in which information will be shared for escalation or exceptional events. Details of the information required by the project team from stakeholders should also be clearly defined.

4.2 Critical Success Factors for the Plan Risk Management Process

The principal criteria for a valid risk management plan are acceptance by the stakeholders, alignment with the internal and external constraints on the project, balance between cost or effort and benefit, and completeness with respect to the needs of the Project Risk Management process. Critical success factors for the Plan Risk Management process are detailed below.

4.2.1 Identify and Address Barriers to Successful Project Risk Management

The time and effort required to carry out the Plan Risk Management process will not be supported unless the stakeholders, and especially management in the organization responsible for the project, recognize and accept the benefits of managing risk, and the added value of addressing this as a skill in its own right rather than as a passive or reactive component of general project management.

A clear definition of the project objectives and a high-level view of the project environment and solution approach are required to provide a valid basis for risk management. The project manager should therefore ensure that valid definition and planning information is available for the plan risk management activity.

An organization inexperienced in risk management planning may need to develop its own approach and may expend an inappropriate amount of time and effort on this. Alternatively it may use a proprietary or pre-existing approach which requires tailoring. The availability of some or all of the following organizational process assets contributes to the chances of success of the Plan Risk Management activities: standard templates, predefined risk categories, and an established project management methodology incorporating risk management procedures that specify what risk information is required for decision making, when it is required, and a definition of concepts and terms, roles, responsibilities, and authority levels. Access to relevant lessons learned at this stage will allow this experience to be taken into account from the start of the project.

The risk management plan will not deliver its value unless Project Risk Management is carried out as an integral part of the project. The corresponding activities should be built into the project work breakdown structure and included in the corresponding schedule, budget, and work-assignment documents.

4.2.2 Involve Project Stakeholders in Project Risk Management

The project manager needs to involve the project stakeholders in the Plan Risk Management activities to build on their skills and experience as well as to ensure their understanding of, and commitment to, the full Project Risk Management process.

The provision for risk management resources specified within the risk management plan should be approved by management at a level adequate for carrying out the required Project Risk Management processes in accordance with agreed-upon objectives. Management should be involved in the analysis of the level of resourcing required for managing project risk and accept the risks that may arise from specific limitations placed on the provision of resources. Disagreements between stakeholders in the areas of risk tolerance and evaluation measures should be addressed and resolved.

4.2.3 Comply with the Organization's Objectives, Policies, and Practices

The feasibility of risk management planning is dependent upon the features of the organization in which it is carried out. The rules and guidelines defined in the risk management plan should be compatible with the culture of the organization, its capabilities from the point of view of people and facilities, and its values, goals, and objectives.

Project management in general, and risk management in particular, contribute to the organization's effective governance. The risk management plan should identify and take into account the relevant organizational procedures and any other enterprise environmental factors that apply such as strategic risk management or corporate governance processes.

4.3 Tools and Techniques for the Plan Risk Management Process

4.3.1 Planning Sessions

Planning sessions are recommended in order to build a common understanding of the project's risk approach between project stakeholders and to gain agreement on the techniques to be used for managing risk.

Elaboration of the risk management plan often serves to develop an effective means for the team to work together since a similar consultative team approach will be used in subsequent stages of the risk management process. The participants should include: the project manager, selected project team members and other stakeholders, members of the broader organization having responsibility for risk, and other subject matter experts or facilitators, as needed.

At this point, the initial risk responsibilities, methodology, templates, terms, definitions, time schedules, and cost budgets for the other Project Risk Management processes should be assigned and accepted. The specification for the tools that will be used in subsequent processes should include all parameters and other inputs required to ensure their applicability to the specific project. These should be documented in the risk management plan, which, when formally approved, is the principal deliverable of the Plan Risk Management process.

4.3.2 Templates

In order to benefit from experience and existing best practice, risk management planning should take into account relevant existing templates for work products, such as risk status reports, risk breakdown structures or the risk register. A decision should be made as to which templates are relevant to the project, and these should then be adapted and included in the risk management plan.

4.4 Documenting the Results of the Plan Risk Management Process

The results of risk management planning are documented in the risk management plan. The plan serves to provide all project stakeholders with a common view of how the risk-related activities of the project will be handled, what has been agreed upon, and a description of the stakeholders' involvement and responsibilities in these activities. An overview of the key areas of focus is given in Figure 4-1.

People	Tools	Business
Attitudes	Toolbox	Constraints
Roles, responsibilities, authority	Parameters	Amount of detail and effort
Communications	Definitions	

Figure 4-1. Key Areas of Focus for the Plan Risk Management Process

Depending upon the size and complexity of the project, some or all of the following elements will be present in a risk management plan.

- Introduction;
- Project description;
- Risk management methodology;
- Risk management organization;
- Roles, responsibilities, and authority;
- Stakeholder risk tolerance;
- Criteria for success;
- Risk management tools and guidelines for use;
- Thresholds and corresponding definitions;
- Templates;
- Communications plan;
- Strategy; and
- Risk breakdown structure.

CHAPTER 5

IDENTIFY RISKS

5.1 Purpose and Objectives of the Identify Risks Process

A risk cannot be managed unless it is first identified. Consequently, after risk management planning has been completed, the first process in the iterative Project Risk Management process aims to identify all the knowable risks to project objectives.

It is, however, impossible to identify all the risks at the outset of a project. Over time, the level of project risk exposure changes as a result of the decisions and actions taken previously in the project (internal change) and of externally imposed change.

The purpose of risk identification is to identify risks to the maximum extent that is practicable. The fact that some risks are unknowable or emergent requires the Identify Risk process to be iterative, repeating the Identify Risks process to find new risks which have become knowable since the previous iteration of the process.

When a risk is first identified, potential responses may also be identified at the same time. These should be recorded during the Identify Risks process and considered for immediate action if such action is appropriate. Where such responses are not implemented immediately, these should be considered during the Plan Risk Responses process.

5.2 Critical Success Factors for the Identify Risks Process

The practices described in Sections 5.2.1 through 5.2.10 will maximize the value and effectiveness of the Identify Risks process and enhance the likelihood of identifying as many risks as practicable.

5.2.1 Early Identification

Risk identification should be performed as early as possible in the project lifecycle, recognizing the paradox that uncertainty is high in the initial stages of a project so there is often less information on which to base the risk identification. Early risk identification enables key project decisions to take maximum account of risks inherent in the project, and may result in changes to the project strategy. It also maximizes the time available for development and implementation of risk responses, which enhances efficiency since responses taken early are often normally less costly than later ones.

5.2.2 Iterative Identification

Since not all risks can be identified at any given point in the project, it is essential that risk identification is repeated throughout the project life cycle. This should be done periodically, at a frequency determined during the Plan Risk Management process. Risk identification might also be repeated at key milestones in the project, or whenever there is significant change to the project or its operating environment.

5.2.3 Emergent Identification

In addition to invoking the Identify Risks process as defined in the project plan, the Project Risk Management process should permit risks to be identified at any time, not limited to formal risk identification events or regular reviews.

5.2.4 Comprehensive Identification

A broad range of sources of risk should be considered to ensure that as many uncertainties as possible that might affect objectives have been identified.

5.2.5 Explicit Identification of Opportunities

The Identify Risks process should ensure opportunities are properly considered.

5.2.6 Multiple Perspectives

The Identify Risks process should take input from a broad range of project stakeholders to ensure that all perspectives are represented and considered. Limiting risk identification to the immediate project team is unlikely to expose all knowable risks.

5.2.7 Risks Linked to Project Objectives

Each identified project risk should relate to at least one project objective (time, cost, quality, scope, etc.), noting that the *PMBOK® Guide* defines risk as an uncertain event or condition that, if it occurs, has a positive or a negative effect on a project's objectives. Consideration of each project objective during the Identify Risks process will assist in identifying risks, noting that some risks may affect more than one objective.

5.2.8 Complete Risk Statement

Identified risks should be clearly and unambiguously described, so that they can be understood by those responsible for risk assessment and risk response planning. Single words or phrases such as "resources" or "logistics" are inadequate and do not properly communicate the nature of the risk. More detailed risk descriptions are required which explicitly state the uncertainty and its causes and effects.

5.2.9 Ownership and Level of Detail

Risks can be identified at a number of levels of detail. A generalized or high-level description of risk can make it difficult to develop responses and assign ownership, while describing risks in a lot of detail can create a great deal of work. Each risk should be described at a level of detail at which it can be assigned to a single risk owner with clear responsibility and accountability for its management. Trigger conditions should also be identified where this is possible and appropriate.

5.2.10 Objectivity

All human activities are susceptible to bias, especially when dealing with uncertainty. Both motivational biases, where someone is trying to bias the result in one direction or another, or cognitive biases, where biases occur as people are using their best judgment and applying heuristics, may occur. This should be explicitly recognized and addressed during the Identify Risks process. Sources of bias should be exposed wherever possible, and their effect on the risk process should be managed proactively. The aim is to minimize subjectivity, and allow open and honest identification of as many risks as possible to the project.

5.3 Tools and Techniques for the Identify Risks Process

A range of tools and techniques is available for risk identification. These fall into the following three categories, as illustrated in Figure 5-1:

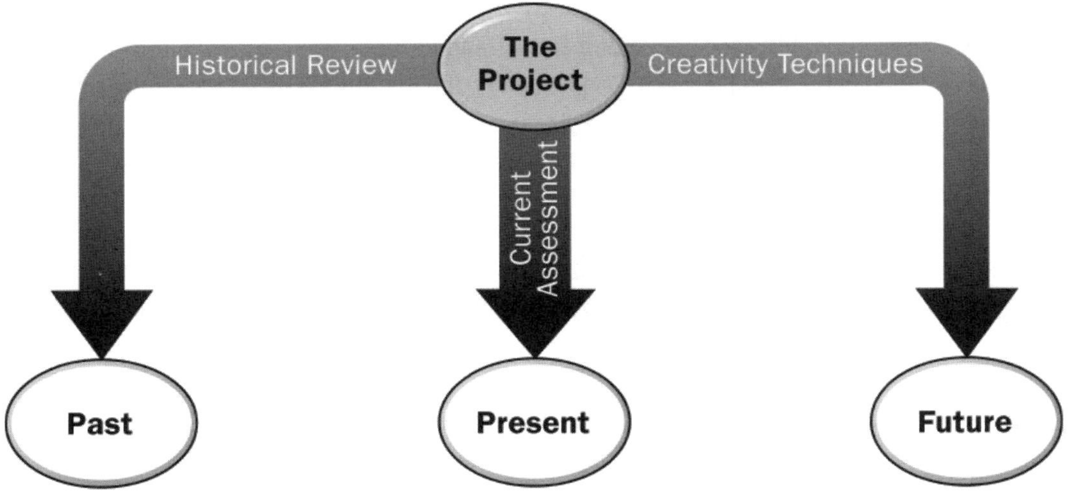

Figure 5-1. Three Perspectives of Risk Identification

5.3.1 Historical Review

Historical reviews are based on what occurred in the past, either on this project, or other similar projects in the same organization, or comparable projects in other organizations. Historical review approaches rely on careful selection of comparable situations which are genuinely similar to the current project, and filtering of data to ensure that only relevant previous risks are considered. In each case, the risks identified in the selected historical situation should be considered, asking whether they or similar risks might arise in this project.

5.3.2 Current Assessments

Current assessments rely on detailed consideration of the current project, analyzing its characteristics against given frameworks and models in order to expose areas of uncertainty. Unlike historical review approaches, current assessment techniques do not rely on outside reference points, but are based purely on examination of the project.

5.3.3 Creativity Techniques

A wide range of creativity techniques can be used for risk identification, which encourages project stakeholders to use their imagination to find risks which might affect the project. The outcomes or effectiveness of these techniques depend on the ability of participants to think creatively. These techniques can be used either singly or in groups, and employ varying degrees of structure. These techniques depend on the ability of participants to think creatively, and their success is enhanced by use of a skilled facilitator.

Each category of risk identification technique has strengths and weaknesses, and no single technique can be expected to reveal all knowable risks. Consequently, the Identify Risks process for a particular project should use a combination of techniques, perhaps selecting one from each category. For example, a project may choose to use a risk identification checklist (historical review), together with assumptions analysis (current assessment) and brainstorming (creativity).

Use of a risk breakdown structure which organizes the categories of potential risks on the project, a prompt list, or a set of generic list categories may assist in ensuring that as many sources of risk as practicable have been addressed, while recognizing that no such tools are complete nor can they replace original thinking.

Whichever risk identification techniques are used, it is important that identified risks are unambiguously described in order to ensure that the project risk process is focused on the actual risks and not distracted or diluted by non-risks. Use of structured risk descriptions can ensure clarity. Risk meta-language offers a useful way of distinguishing a risk from its cause(s) and effect(s), describing each risk using three-part statements in the form: "As a result of cause, risk may occur, which would lead to effect." The relationship between cause, risk, and effect is shown in Figure 5-2.

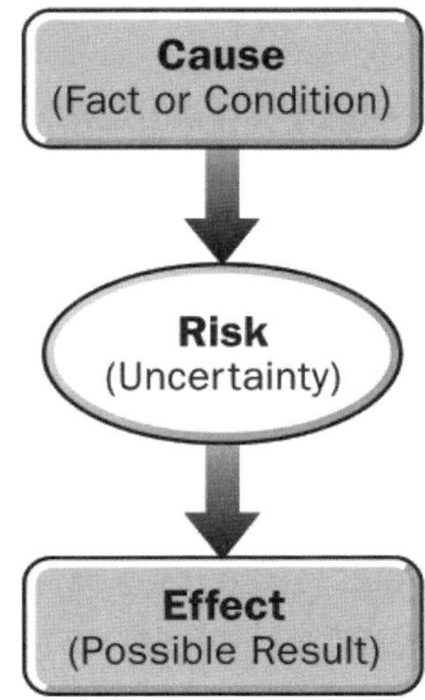

Figure 5-2. Cause, Risk, and Effect

5.4 Documenting the Results of the Identify Risks Process

The results from the Identify Risks process should be recorded in order to capture all relevant information currently available for each identified risk. The main output from the Identify Risks process is the risk register. This includes a properly structured risk description and the nominated risk owner for each risk, and may also include information on the causes and effects of the risk, trigger conditions, and preliminary responses.

CHAPTER 6

PERFORM QUALITATIVE RISK ANALYSIS

6.1 Purpose and Objectives of the Perform Qualitative Risk Analysis Process

The Perform Qualitative Risk Analysis process assesses and evaluates characteristics of individually identified project risks and prioritizes risks based on agreed-upon characteristics.

Assessing individual risks using qualitative risk analysis evaluates the probability that each risk will occur and the effect of each individual risk on the project objectives. As such it does not directly address the overall risk to project objectives that results from the combined effect of all risks and their potential interactions with each other. This can however be achieved through use of quantitative risk analysis techniques (see Chapter 7).

One step in the analysis is to categorize risks according to their sources or causes. If several risks arise from a common source, sometimes called a root cause, risk responses may be more effective when they focus on addressing this root cause.

Identifying common effects from groups of risks allows identification of the areas of greatest risk exposure (e.g. to the project completion date, the budget, or a particular deliverable's scope), facilitating risk response focus in these areas.

The methods of qualitative risk analysis are applied to the list of risks created or updated by the Identify Risks process to provide project management with the characteristics of the risks that have the most influence (positive or negative) on achieving the project's objectives. Risks that are assessed as high priority to either threaten or to enhance the achievement of project objectives will be an important focus in the Plan Risk Responses process. They may be further analyzed, such as in the analysis of the overall project risk that is discussed in Perform Quantitative Risk Analysis process.

6.2 Critical Success Factors for the Perform Qualitative Risk Analysis Process

Several factors that lead to successful qualitative risk analysis are described in Sections 6.2.1 through 6.2.4, and summarized in Figure 6-1. Agreement of the project stakeholders is a fundamental criterion and a common theme. The agreed-upon approach is the foundation of process credibility. Then, agreed-upon definitions enable high-quality information to be collected. Finally, with these conditions in place, the process can be executed reliably, which contributes to the credibility of its outputs.

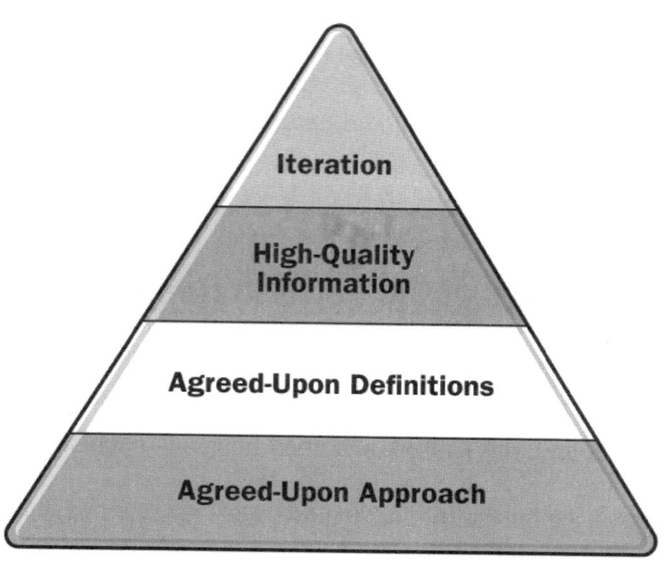

Figure 6-1. Building Risk Analysis Credibility

6.2.1 Use Agreed-Upon Approach

The process is based on an agreed-upon approach to this assessment that is applied across all of the identified risks in any project. By the nature of project risk, all risks may be assessed according to probability of occurrence and impact on individual objectives should the risk occur. Other factors may be considered in determining the importance of a risk as follows:

- **Urgency (proximity).** Risks requiring near term responses may be considered more urgent to address. Indicators of urgency can include the lead time necessary to execute a risk response and the clarity of symptoms and warning signs (also known as detectability) that may trigger the response.
- **Manageability.** Some risks are not manageable and it would be a waste of resources to attempt to address them. The project team may examine these and decide to:
  - Go forward, perhaps establishing a contingency reserve.
  - Stop or re-scope the project because these risks pose an unmanageable threat or an opportunity that should not be missed with high probability and consequences.
  - Inform the customer of the risks and ask for a decision from their point of view.
- **Impact external to the project.** A risk may increase in importance if it affects the enterprise beyond the project.

6.2.2 Use Agreed-Upon Definitions of Risk Terms

The risk assessment should be based on agreed-upon definitions of important terms, and those definitions should be used consistently when assessing each risk. The use of definitions, for example, of levels of probability and of impact on objectives, assists the providers of the information in giving realistic assessments for each risk, and facilitates the communication of the results to management and other stakeholders.

6.2.3 Collect High-Quality Information about Risks

Collection of high-quality information about risks is required. Often this information is not available in any historic database and should be gathered by interviews, workshops, and other means using expert judgment. Data gathered from individuals may be subject to reporting or intentional bias. When this occurs, the bias should be identified and remedied where possible, or a different, unbiased source of information should be found and used.

6.2.4 Perform Iterative Qualitative Risk Analysis

The success of qualitative risk analysis is enhanced if the process is used periodically throughout the project. It is impossible to know in advance all the risks that may occur in a project, therefore the Identify Risks and Perform Qualitative Analysis processes should be repeated periodically for individual risks. The frequency of this effort will be planned in the Plan Risk Management process, but may also depend on events within the project itself.

6.3 Tools and Techniques for the Perform Qualitative Risk Analysis Process

The tools and techniques used for assessing individual risks will identify the risks that are important to the project's success. This process is illustrated in Figure 6-2.

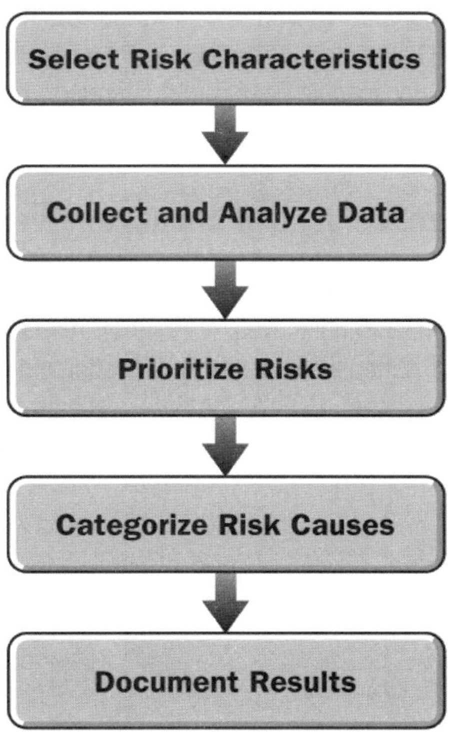

Figure 6-2. The Perform Qualitative Risk Analysis Process

6.3.1 Select Risk Characteristics that Define Risks' Importance

Qualitative risk analysis tools provide ways to distinguish those risks that are important for response or further analysis from those that are less important. The criteria that make a risk of interest to management are agreed upon in advance and implemented in the tools used. Output from qualitative risk analysis tools includes a listing of risks in priority order or in priority groups (e.g., high, moderate, and low).

The tools for qualitative risk analysis allow the organization or project stakeholders to specify those levels or combinations of risk characteristics that make a particular risk of interest to management. Most tools assess a risk's importance from a combination of probability of occurrence and degree of impact on objectives.

6.3.2 Collect and Analyze Data

Assessment of individual risks is based on information collected about them. Therefore, data collection and evaluation tools, including interviews, workshops, and references to databases of prior projects, require management support and attention. It is important to protect against bias in data gathering, which is important when relying on expert judgment for the information.

6.3.3 Prioritize Risks by Probability and Impact on Specific Objectives

Some tools permit distinguishing a risk's priority in terms of the affected objective. This capability provides a list of risks that are important for any specific objective of interest to management. This is useful since it is common for risks to have uneven impacts on various project objectives.

6.3.4 Prioritize Risks by Probability and Impact on Overall Project

There are reasons for constructing a measure of a specific risk's importance to the entire project as contrasted with its importance to specific objectives. A common reason is for ease of communication with management and other stakeholders. When a single risk prioritization index is needed, the organization should be explicit about how that index is created. Usually the index reflects the organization's preference among objectives. The technique for creating the overall risk priority measure should be documented in the Plan Risk Management process.

6.3.5 Categorize Risk Causes

Categorizing risks appropriately may lead to improved analysis of the probability and magnitude of project risk and to effective responses. Understanding the relationships between risks may provide a better understanding of the possibility and magnitude of project risk than if risks are only considered as separate and independent events. Identifying common root causes of a group of risks, for instance, may reveal both the magnitude of the risk event for the group as a whole along with effective strategies that might address several risks simultaneously. Alternatively, some risks may be linked with others in a causal chain, and understanding the chain of risks may lead to a better understanding of the implication of risk for the project. Identifying risks that can occur at the same time or using the same resources for recovery might provide a realistic picture of problems of risk mitigation using scarce resources.

Combining the results of the Perform Qualitative Risk Analysis process with the risk breakdown structure (see Identify Risks, Chapter 5) can show clusters of priority risks arising from specific sources. A combination of the risk analysis information with the work breakdown structure (WBS) can show which areas of the project exhibit the most risk. Assessing the high-priority risks' impact on one objective, such as the schedule, may indicate which activities to address to reduce that objective's uncertainty. All of these approaches can contribute to the realism and usefulness of the qualitative risk analysis.

6.4 Documenting the Results of the Perform Qualitative Risk Analysis Process

The Perform Qualitative Risk Analysis process adds structure to the list of undifferentiated risks (see Identify Risks, Chapter 5) into categories of priority. Priorities are usually based on the risk's probability of occurring and its potential impact on specific project objectives or on the whole project. Each identified risk is assigned a priority, perhaps by objective or for the entire project. This information is usually stored in the risk register which is easy to use and update with new information. The risk register list of prioritized risks is posted to the project participants who are responsible for further analysis or action to improve the project plan. Risks that are judged to have high priority are segregated for further analysis and response planning and are generally monitored frequently. Risks of low priority to the project may be placed on a watch list and are reviewed less often for changes in their status.

CHAPTER 7

PERFORM QUANTITATIVE RISK ANALYSIS

7.1 Purpose and Objectives of the Perform Quantitative Risk Analysis Process

The Perform Quantitative Risk Analysis process provides a numerical estimate of the overall effect of risk on the objectives of the project, based on current plans and information, when considering risks simultaneously. Results from this type of analysis can be used to evaluate the likelihood of success in achieving project objectives and to estimate contingency reserves, usually for time and cost that are appropriate to both the risks and the risk tolerance of project stakeholders.

It is generally accepted that analyzing uncertainty in the project using quantitative techniques such as Monte Carlo simulation may provide more realism in the estimate of the overall project cost or schedule than a non-probabilistic approach which assumes that the activity durations or line-item cost estimates are deterministic. However it should be recognized that quantitative risk analysis is not always required or appropriate for all projects. For example, qualitative risk analysis may provide enough information for development of effective risk responses, especially for smaller projects. Therefore, during the Plan Risk Management process, the benefits of quantitative risk analysis should be weighed against the effort required to ensure that the additional insights and value justify the additional effort.

Partial risk analyses, such as qualitative risk analysis, aim at prioritizing individual risks viewed one at a time and therefore cannot produce measures of overall project risk when all risks are considered simultaneously. Calculating estimates of overall project risk is the focus of the Perform Quantitative Risk Analysis process.

Specific project risks are usually best understood and quantified at a detailed level such as the line-item cost or schedule activity level. By contrast, project objectives such as achievement of the project's budget or the schedule are specified at a higher level, often at the level of the total project. An overall risk analysis, such as one that uses quantitative techniques, estimates the implication of all quantified risks on project objectives. The implementation of overall risk analysis using quantitative methods requires:

- Complete and accurate representation of the project objectives built up from individual project elements. Examples of these representations include the project schedule or cost estimate.
- Identifying risks on individual project elements such as schedule activities or line-item costs at a level of detail that lends itself to specific assessment of individual risks.
- Including generic risks that have a broader effect than individual project elements.
- Applying a quantitative method (such as Monte Carlo simulation or decision tree analysis) that incorporates multiple risks simultaneously in determining overall impact on the overall project objective.

Results of the quantitative analysis will be compared to the project plan (baseline or current) to give management an estimate of the overall project risk and will answer important questions such as:

- What is the probability of meeting the project's objectives?
- How much contingency reserve (e.g., reserves or buffers of time, resources, and cost) is needed to provide the organization with the level of certainty it requires based upon its risk tolerance?
- What are those parts of the project, such as line-item costs or schedule activities, which contribute the most risk when all risks are considered simultaneously?
- Which individual risks contribute the most to overall project risk?

Estimating overall project risk using quantitative methods helps distinguish those projects where quantified risks threaten objectives beyond the tolerance of the stakeholders, from those for which the objectives are within acceptable tolerances even when risk is considered. The former may be targeted for vigorous risk responses aimed at protecting those objectives most important to the stakeholders.

A high-level comparison of quantitative and qualitative risk analysis processes is presented in Figure 7-1.

Qualitative Risk Analysis	Quantitative Risk Analysis
• Addresses individual risks descriptively • Assesses the discrete probability of occurrence and impact on objectives if it does occur • Prioritizes individual risks for subsequent treatment • Adds to risk register • Leads to quantitative risk analysis	• Predicts likely project outcomes based on combined effects of risks • Uses probability distributions to characterize the risk's probability and impact • Uses project model (e.g. schedule, cost estimate) • Uses a quantitative method, requires specialized tools • Estimates likelihood of meeting targets and contingency needed to achieve desired level of comfort • Identifies risks with greatest effect on overall project risk

Figure 7-1. Comparison of Qualitative and Quantitative Approaches

7.2 Critical Success Factors for the Perform Quantitative Risk Analysis Process

Success in achieving the objectives of quantitative risk analysis depends explicitly on at least the factors described in Sections 7.2.1 through 7.2.6.

7.2.1 Prior Risk Identification and Qualitative Risk Analysis

The Perform Quantitative Risk Analysis process occurs after the Identify Risks and Perform Qualitative Risk Analysis processes have been completed. Reference to a prioritized list of identified risks ensures that the Perform Quantitative Risk Analysis process will consider all significant risks when analyzing their effects quantitatively.

7.2.2 Appropriate Project Model

An appropriate model of the project should be used as the basis for quantitative risk analysis. Project models most frequently used in quantitative risk analysis include the project schedule (for time), line-item cost estimates (for cost), decision tree (for decisions in the face of uncertainty) and other total-project models. Quantitative risk analysis is especially sensitive to the completeness and correctness of the model of the project that is used.

7.2.3 Commitment to Collecting High-Quality Risk Data

Often high-quality data about risks are not available in any historic database and should be gathered by interviews, workshops, and other means using expert judgment of those present. Collection of risk data requires resources and time as well as management support.

7.2.4 Unbiased Data

Success in gathering risk analysis data requires the ability to recognize when biases occur and combating that bias or developing other unbiased sources of the data. Bias in risk data can occur for many reasons, but two common sources of bias are cognitive bias and motivational bias.

7.2.5 Overall Project Risk Derived from Individual Risks

The Perform Quantitative Risk Analysis process is based upon a methodology that correctly derives the overall project risk from the individual risks. In risk analysis of cost and schedule, for example, an appropriate method is Monte Carlo simulation. A decision tree is an appropriate method for making decisions when future events are not certain, using the probability and impact of all risks, and combining their effect to derive an overall project measure such as value or cost. In each of these methods, the risks are specified at the level of the detailed tasks or line-item costs and incorporated into the model of the project to calculate effects on objectives such as schedule or cost for the entire project, by combining those risks.

7.2.6 Interrelationships Between Risks in Quantitative Risk Analysis

Attention should be given to the possibility that the individual risks in the project model are related to each other. For example, several risks may have a common root cause and therefore are likely to occur together. This possibility is sometimes addressed by correlating the risks that are related, ensuring that they generally occur together during the analysis. Another common way to represent the risks which occur together is by using the risk register listing of the risk or root cause and attaching it to several project elements such as schedule activities or cost elements. When a particular risk occurs, the affected elements will all experience the effect of that risk together.

7.3 Tools and Techniques for the Perform Quantitative Risk Analysis Process

Tools and techniques used appropriately for quantitative risk analysis have several characteristics, as follows:

7.3.1 Comprehensive Risk Representation

Risk models permit representation of many, if not all, of the risks that have impact on an objective simultaneously. They also permit the representation of both opportunities and threats to the project's objectives.

7.3.2 Risk Impact Calculation

Quantitative models facilitate the correct calculation of the effect of many risks, which are typically identified and quantified at a level of detail below the total project, on the project objectives, which are typically described at the level of the total project.

7.3.3 Quantitative Method Appropriate to Analyzing Uncertainty

Probability models use a quantitative method that addresses uncertainty. Specifically, the methods should be able to handle the way uncertainty is represented, predominantly as probability of an event's occurring or as probability distributions for a range of outcomes. A good example of this is the use of Monte Carlo simulation tools that permit the combination of probability distributions of line-item costs or schedule activity durations, many of which are uncertain.

7.3.4 Data Gathering Tools

Data gathering tools used in this process include assessment of historical data and workshops, interviews, or questionnaires to gather quantified information—for example, on the probability of a risk occurring, a probability distribution of its potential impacts on cost or time, or relationships such as correlation between risks.

7.3.5 Effective Presentation of Quantitative Analysis Results

Results from the quantitative tools are generally not available in standard deterministic project management methods such as project scheduling or cost estimating. Examples of these are the probability distribution of project completion dates or total costs and the expected value of a project decision. These results, when all risks are considered simultaneously, include the following:

- Probability of achieving a project objective such as finishing on time or within budget.
- Amount of contingency reserve in cost, time, or resources needed to provide a required level of confidence.
- Identity or location within the project model of the most important risks. An example of this is a sensitivity analysis in a cost risk analysis or a criticality analysis in a schedule risk analysis.

The elements of a quantitative risk analysis are illustrated in Figure 7-2.

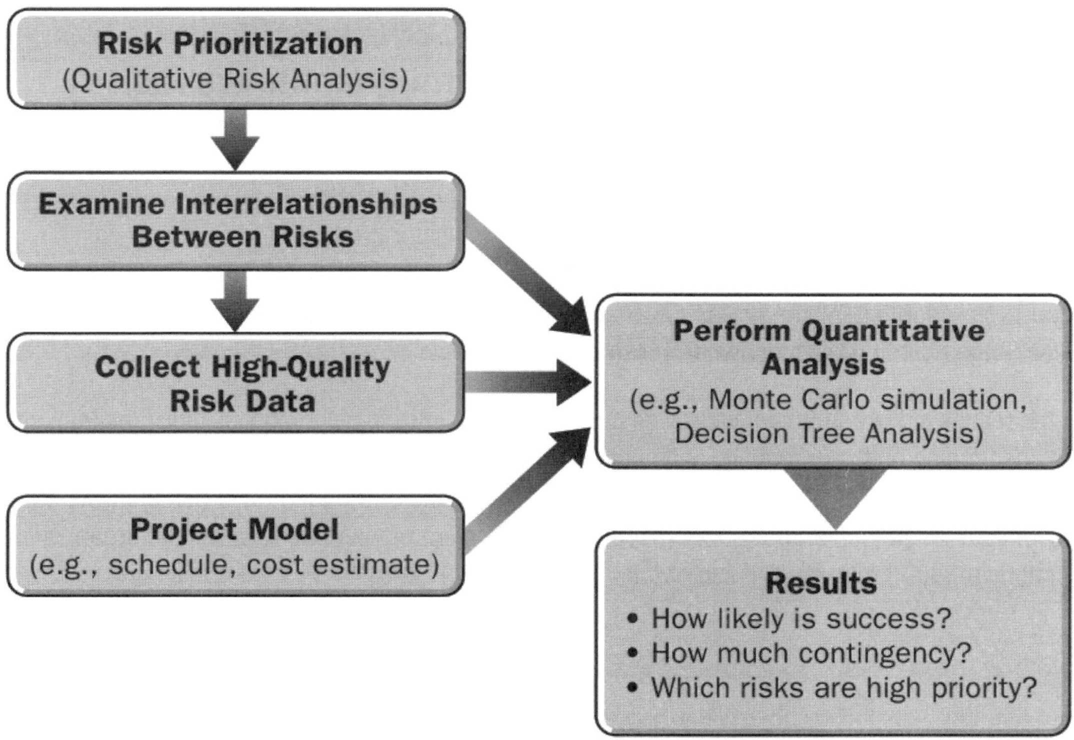

Figure 7-2. Structure of a Quantitative Risk Analysis

7.3.6 Iterative Quantitative Risk Analysis

The success of the Perform Quantitative Risk Analysis process is enhanced if the process is used periodically throughout the project. It is impossible to know in advance all of the risks that may occur in a project. Often quantitative risk analysis should be repeated as the project proceeds. The frequency of this effort will be determined during the Plan Risk Management process but will also depend on events within the project itself (see Monitor and Control Risks, Chapter 9).

7.3.7 Information for Response Planning

Overall project contingency reserve in time and cost should be reflected in the project's schedule and budget. Quantitative risk analysis provides information that may be used to modify the project plan. If the overall risk to time and cost indicates that an adjustment in scope is needed, the scope changes are agreed upon and documented and a new quantitative risk analysis is carried out to reflect the new aspects of the project.

7.4 Documenting the Results of the Perform Quantitative Risk Analysis Process

The contingency reserves calculated in quantitative project cost and schedule risk analysis are incorporated, respectively, into the cost estimate and the schedule to establish a prudent target and a realistic expectation for the project. Contingency reserves may also be established to provide for the capture of opportunities that are judged to be priorities for the project. If the contingency reserve required exceeds the time or resources available, changes in the project scope and plan may result.

Also, the results of the analysis may provide more or less urgency to risk response (see Plan Risk Responses, Chapter 8) depending on the probability of achieving the plan's objectives or the amount of contingency reserve required to provide the necessary level of confidence. The results of a quantitative risk analysis are recorded and passed on to the person and/or group responsible for project management within the organization for any further actions required to make full use of these results.

CHAPTER 8

PLAN RISK RESPONSES

The Plan Risk Responses process determines effective response actions that are appropriate to the priority of the individual risks and to the overall project risk. It takes into account the stakeholders' risk attitudes and the conventions specified in the Risk Management Plan, in addition to any constraints and assumptions that were determined when the risks were identified and analyzed.

8.1 Purpose and Objectives of the Plan Risk Responses Process

The objective of the Plan Risk Responses process is to determine the set of actions which most enhance the chances of project success while complying with applicable organizational and project constraints.

Once risks have been identified, analyzed, and prioritized, plans should be developed for addressing every risk the project team considers to be sufficiently important, either because of the threat it poses to the project objectives or the opportunity it offers. The planning entails agreeing upon the actions to be taken and the potential changes to budget, schedule, resources, and scope which these actions might cause.

Contingent risk response actions need to be executed at the optimum time. For this reason, the response specification for each such risk should include a description of any corresponding trigger conditions.

The responsibility for monitoring the project conditions and implementing the corresponding actions should be clearly assigned. Every risk should have been allocated to a risk owner as part of the Identify Risks process, and each of the corresponding risk responses should now be assigned to a specific risk action owner. The risk owner is responsible for ensuring that the risk response is effective and for planning additional risk responses if required, whereas the risk action owner is responsible for ensuring that the agreed-upon risk responses are carried out as planned, in a timely manner. The role of the risk owner and that of the risk action owner may be assigned to a single person.

Responses, when implemented, can have potential effects on the project objectives and, as such, can generate additional risks. These are known as secondary risks and have to be analyzed and planned for in the same way as those risks which were initially identified.

It is never feasible or even desirable to eliminate all threats from a project. Similarly, there is also a limit to the extent to which opportunities can be proactively managed. There may be residual risks that will remain after the responses have been implemented. These residual risks should be clearly identified, analyzed, documented, and communicated to all relevant stakeholders.

All the approved, unconditional actions arising from risk response planning should be integrated into the project management plan in order to ensure that they are carried out as part of normal project implementation. The corresponding organizational and project management rules should also be invoked, including the following:

- Project change management and configuration control;
- Project planning, budgeting, and scheduling;
- Resource management; and
- Project communication planning.

8.2 Critical Success Factors for the Plan Risk Responses Process

A range of factors are important for the success of the Plan Risk Responses process. These are described in Sections 8.2.1 through 8.2.8 and shown in Figure 8-1.

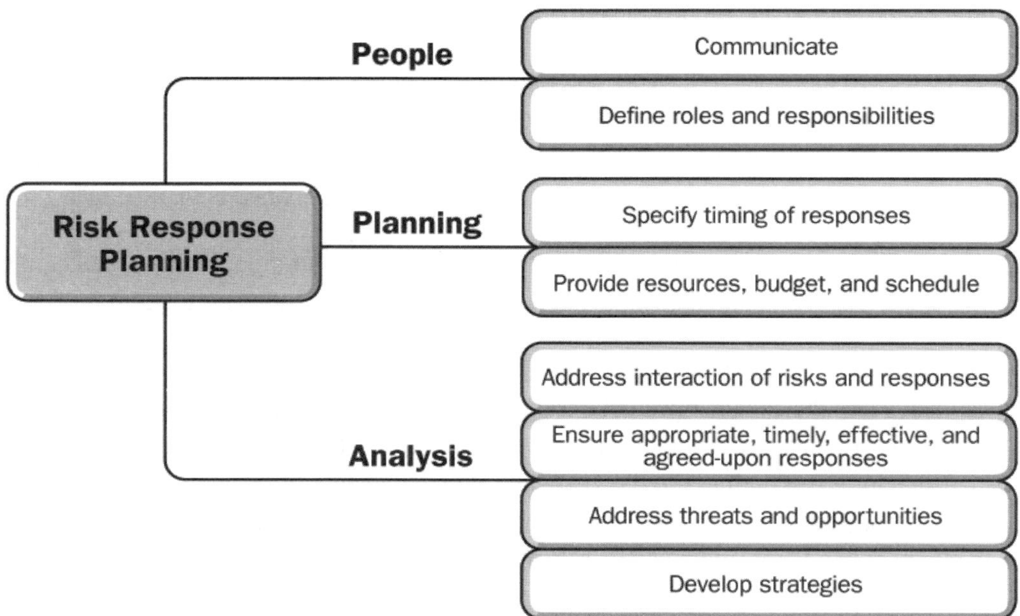

Figure 8-1. Critical Success Factors for Risk Response Planning

8.2.1 Communicate

Communication with the various stakeholders should be maintained in an open and appropriate manner. The resulting plans are disseminated and approval obtained in order to ensure full acceptance by all stakeholders.

In addition, if organizational causes of risks, such as culture, attitudes, or disagreements concerning objectives are present, they should be addressed openly. This may require involving high levels of the organization's management and other stakeholders.

8.2.2 Clearly Define Risk-Related Roles and Responsibilities

The risk response success will be dependent upon the full support and involvement of the project team and other stakeholders. The key roles for Project Risk Management are those of risk owner and risk action owner. A single risk owner should be assigned to every identified risk, and each agreed-upon risk response should have a single risk action owner. The people with the corresponding responsibilities should be aware of what is expected of them, and the other project stakeholders should understand and accept the needs and authority of these roles.

Management may take ownership of risks with political, organizational causes. In addition, senior management should approve and track associated risk-related contingency reserves.

8.2.3 Specify Timing of Risk Responses

Agreed-upon responses should be integrated into the project management plan and will therefore be scheduled and assigned for execution. The responses that depend on uncertain conditions should also be monitored so as to be performed if the conditions warrant them.

8.2.4 Provide Resources, Budget, and Schedule for Responses

Each response should be planned in detail in accordance with the methodology of the project and integrated into the project management plan. This entails estimating the resources, costs, and duration; updating the budget and schedule; obtaining approval from management; and obtaining commitment from the risk owners and risk action owners. Management's role at this stage is vital for supporting the project manager in developing risk responses and authorizing the corresponding resources.

8.2.5 Address the Interaction of Risks and Responses

Responses may be developed to address risks related either by cause and effect or by common root cause. Categorization of risks, for example by using tools such as the risk breakdown structure, affinity diagram, or other categorizing tools, may help identify and address this situation. There is also a need during the Plan Risk Responses process to consider the risks aggregated during the Perform Quantitative Risk Analysis process (e.g., ten small, related risks combined may pose a big risk to the project), and then to develop generic responses where possible. Another interaction effect that may occur is when one risk, if it occurs, may affect the probability or impact of other risks.

Deciding on the response strategy may require a compromise, since some proposed responses may be mutually exclusive or counterproductive. For example mitigating a threat to time could cost money, thereby increasing pressure on the budget. Risk response planning also needs to take a holistic view of all proposed responses and make sure they are coherent.

The challenge therefore in planning responses to risks is the need to control the potential effects of the strategy developed for treating the original risk. If this is overlooked, the total level of threat in a project can actually increase, or the potential for opportunities can be compromised.

8.2.6 Ensure Appropriate, Timely, Effective, and Agreed-Upon Responses

In general, responses should be appropriate, timely, cost-effective, feasible, achievable, agreed-upon, assigned, and accepted. Any proposed risk response plan needs to be assessed against the following criteria:

- Consistency with organizational values, project objectives, and stakeholder expectations;
- Technical feasibility;
- Ability of the project team or risk action owners outside the project to carry out the corresponding actions; and
- Balance between overall impact of the response on the project objectives and the improvement in the risk profile of the project.

8.2.7 Address Both Threats and Opportunities

Risk response planning should combine responses that address the threats as well as those that provide for opportunities into a single, integrated plan. If either threats or opportunities are not fully addressed, the combined set of response strategies will be incomplete and may even be invalid.

8.2.8 Develop Strategies before Tactical Responses

Risk response planning should be carried out in an open-minded manner rather than adopting the first response that seems to be feasible. The responses should be planned at a general, strategic level and the strategy validated and agreed upon, prior to developing the detailed tactical approach.

Once the responses have been planned at a strategic level, they should be expanded into actions at the tactical level and integrated into the project management plan (e.g., schedule, budget, and resource assignments). This activity may generate additional secondary risks, which will need to be addressed at this time.

8.3 Risk Response Strategies

The project manager should develop risk response strategies for individual risks, sets of risks, and project-level risks. An overview of the steps in arriving at a complete set of responses is given in Figure 8-2.

The affected stakeholders should be involved in determining the strategies. Once the strategies have been selected, they need to be agreed upon by the entity that approves those strategies. There are four strategies which address individual risks for threats and opportunities as described in Sections 8.3.1 through 8.3.4 (see also Fig. 8-2).

8.3.1 Avoid a Threat or Exploit an Opportunity

This strategy involves taking the actions required to address a threat or an opportunity in order to ensure either that the threat cannot occur or can have no effect on the project, or that the opportunity will occur and the project will be able to take advantage of it.

8.3.2 Transfer a Threat or Share an Opportunity

This strategy entails transference to a third party that is better positioned to address a particular threat or opportunity.

8.3.3 Mitigate a Threat or Enhance an Opportunity

Mitigation and enhancement are the most widely applicable and widely used response strategies. Here, the approach is to identify actions that will decrease the probability and/or the impact of a threat, and increase the probability and/or the impact of an opportunity.

8.3.4 Accept a Threat or an Opportunity

This strategy applies when the other strategies are not considered applicable or feasible. Acceptance entails taking no action unless the risk actually occurs, in which case contingency or fallback plans may be developed ahead of time, to be implemented if the risk presents itself.

8.3.5 Applying Risk Response Strategies to Overall Project Risk

In addition to responding to individual risks, the four risk response strategies can be applied to address overall project risk as follows:

- Cancel the project, as a last resort, if the overall level of risk remains unacceptable.
- Set up a business structure in which the customer and the supplier share the risk.
- Re-plan the project or change the scope and boundaries of the project, for example, by modifying the project priority, resource allocations, delivery calendar, etc.
- Pursue the project despite a risk exposure that exceeds the desired level.

8.4 Tools and Techniques for the Plan Risk Responses Process

There are four categories of tools and techniques, as follows:

- Creativity tools to identify potential responses,
- Decision-support tools for determining the optimal potential response.
- Strategy implementation techniques designed to turn a strategy into action, and
- Tools to transfer control to the Monitor and Control Risks process.

These categories of tools can be used respectively to identify potential responses, select the most appropriate response, translate strategy into planning, and assign the corresponding actions. The steps involved in planning risk responses are shown in Figure 8.2.

8.4.1 Response Identification

Risk response planning builds on the available information about the potential risks and aims to determine the optimal set of responses. For this reason, it should involve subject matter experts and employ creativity techniques in order to explore all of the options. Project planning and execution techniques are then required to evaluate the potential effects of the various options on the project's objectives.

8.4.2 Response Selection

Once the set of potential responses for the risks being addressed is established, decision-support techniques may need to be applied to select the best possible subset from these responses. The selection process should take into account the cost of the responses, the impact on the project objectives, uncertainty of outcomes and the possible secondary and residual risks. The Identify Risks, Perform Quantitative Risk Analysis, and Plan Risk Responses processes may then need to be applied to the resultant project management plan and the residual and secondary risks that it would entail. This iterative approach continues until all of the individual risks are deemed acceptable and the overall risk is within a predefined threshold.

8.4.3 Action Planning

Project planning tools are used to turn the chosen strategies into concrete actions and to integrate these into existing plans. The corresponding actions may be unconditional (i.e., integrated into the project management plan) or contingent on a trigger condition and predefined as a contingency response strategy.

8.4.4 Ownership and Responsibility Assignment

The project manager needs to use resource assignment processes to ensure the availability of an owner for each risk and for each response action, so that each associated risk is managed and each corresponding risk response is carried out in a timely and effective manner.

To enable risk monitoring to identify the imminence or actual occurrence of the corresponding event, every contingency response strategy should include a set of trigger conditions. The responsibility for monitoring these conditions should be clearly assigned in the Plan Risk Responses process and managed in the Monitor and Control Risks process.

The strategic definition of risk responses should include measurable criteria for success of the response. Risk action owners should monitor their assigned risks, take agreed-upon actions as required, and provide the risk owners with relevant information on status or changes to the risk characteristics. Risk owners should assess the effectiveness of any actions, decide whether additional actions are required, and keep the project manager informed of the situation.

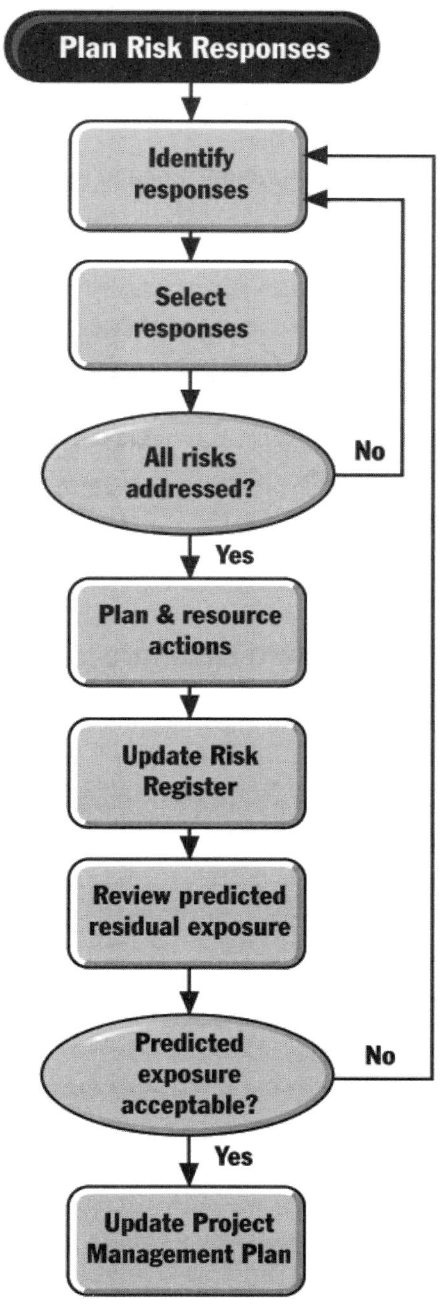

Figure 8-2. The Steps Involved in Planning Risk Responses

8.5 Documenting the Results of the Plan Risk Responses Process

Risk response planning is based on the information placed in the risk register during execution of the Identify Risks and Perform Analysis processes. The corresponding risk response information is often referred to as the risk response plan, although it may in fact be an integral part of the risk register.

8.5.1 Add Risk Responses to the Risk Register

The response-related information for each risk is recorded in the risk register and updated regularly. Any interested stakeholder should be able to rapidly access all the information required to verify their responsibilities and manage the risk in accordance with the risk response plan. The set of residual risks and their priorities are clearly identified and recorded.

8.5.2 Add Corresponding Risk Responses to the Project Management Plan

While developing the detailed set of risk responses, the project-related implications are evaluated for inclusion in a modified project management plan. These include costs, resource assignments, scheduling details, and changes to project documentation. Until these changes are formally approved along with the additional risks that they may carry, risk response planning cannot be considered complete.

8.5.3 Review and Document Predicted Exposure

Once the risk responses have been defined and integrated into the project management plan, the individual and overall residual risks related to this plan are evaluated in order to determine whether additional response planning is required, as shown in Figure 8-2. This evaluation should provide an estimate of both the expected post-response situation and the potential improvement of the risk exposure assuming that the proposed responses are effective. The evaluation should be documented.

CHAPTER 9

MONITOR AND CONTROL RISKS

The effectiveness of Project Risk Management depends upon the way the approved plans are carried out. These plans should be executed correctly, reviewed, and updated regularly. If this is carried out correctly, the invested effort will be rewarded and future projects will benefit from this project's experience.

9.1 Purpose and Objectives of the Monitor and Control Risks Process

The primary objectives of risk monitoring and controlling are to track identified risks, monitor residual risks, identify new risks, ensure that risk response plans are executed at the appropriate time, and evaluate their effectiveness throughout the project life cycle.

In addition to tracking and managing the risk response actions, the effectiveness of all of the Project Risk Management processes should be reviewed to provide improvements to the management of the current project as well as future ones.

For each risk or set of risks for which a contingent response has been defined, the corresponding set of trigger conditions should have been specified. It is the responsibility of the action owner to ensure that these conditions are effectively monitored and that the corresponding actions are carried out as defined, in a timely manner.

Once the Plan Risk Responses process is complete, all of the approved unconditional response actions should have been included and defined in the current project management plan. The first action of risk monitoring and controlling is to check whether this is the case and take any appropriate action if necessary, such as invoking the change management process with respect to any missing actions. This will then ensure that the agreed-upon actions are carried out within the normal project execution framework.

The risk owners and risk action owners need to be briefed on any changes that may affect their responsibilities. Effective communication needs to be maintained between them and the project manager so that the designated stakeholders accept accountability for controlling the potential outcomes of specific risks, apply their best efforts to track the associated trigger conditions and carry out the agreed-upon responses in a timely manner.

In addition to the response actions and trigger conditions, a mechanism for measuring the effectiveness of the response is provided by the Plan Risk Responses process. The risk action owner should keep the risk owner aware of the status of the response actions so that the risk owner can decide when the risk has been effectively dealt with, or whether additional actions need to be planned and implemented.

As the project progresses, additional information becomes available and the project environment may change as some risks occur, whether foreseen or unforeseen, and others become or cease to be relevant. The planning should therefore be kept current and the project manager should ensure that periodic risk reassessment, including risk identification, analysis, and response planning, is repeated at reasonable intervals, or in response to project events—without generating excessive administrative overhead. Typical reasons for risk reassessment are:

- Occurrence of a major or unexpected risk,
- Need to analyze a complex change request,
- Phase end review,
- Project re-planning or major plan elaboration, and
- Periodic review to ensure that the information remains current.

In the event of major organizational changes, risk management planning may need to be revisited prior to reassessing the risks.

In addition to the regular status reviews, periodic audits should be performed to determine strengths and weaknesses in handling risks within the project. This should entail identifying any barriers to effectiveness or keys to success in risk management, recognition of which could lead to improvements in risk management of the current or future projects.

At the end of the project, an integrated analysis of the risk management process should be carried out with a focus on long-term process improvements. This analysis consolidates the findings of the periodic audits to identify lessons that would be applicable in general to a large proportion of the organization's projects in the future, such as appropriate levels of resources, adequate time for the analysis, use of tools, level of detail, etc.

At project closure, the project manager should ensure that a description has been given of the closure of every risk in the risk register, for example: (a) did not occur; (b) occurred and contingency plan invoked; or (c) occurred and impact to the project scope (i.e., time, cost, and quality).

The output of the audit of the risk management process should be consolidated with specific information with respect to the project's experience of risks, and any generally applicable guidelines for the organization should be highlighted and potential actions proposed for applying them. This can lead to an update to the corresponding organizational process assets.

An overview of the steps involved in the Monitor and Control Risks process is given in Figure 9-1.

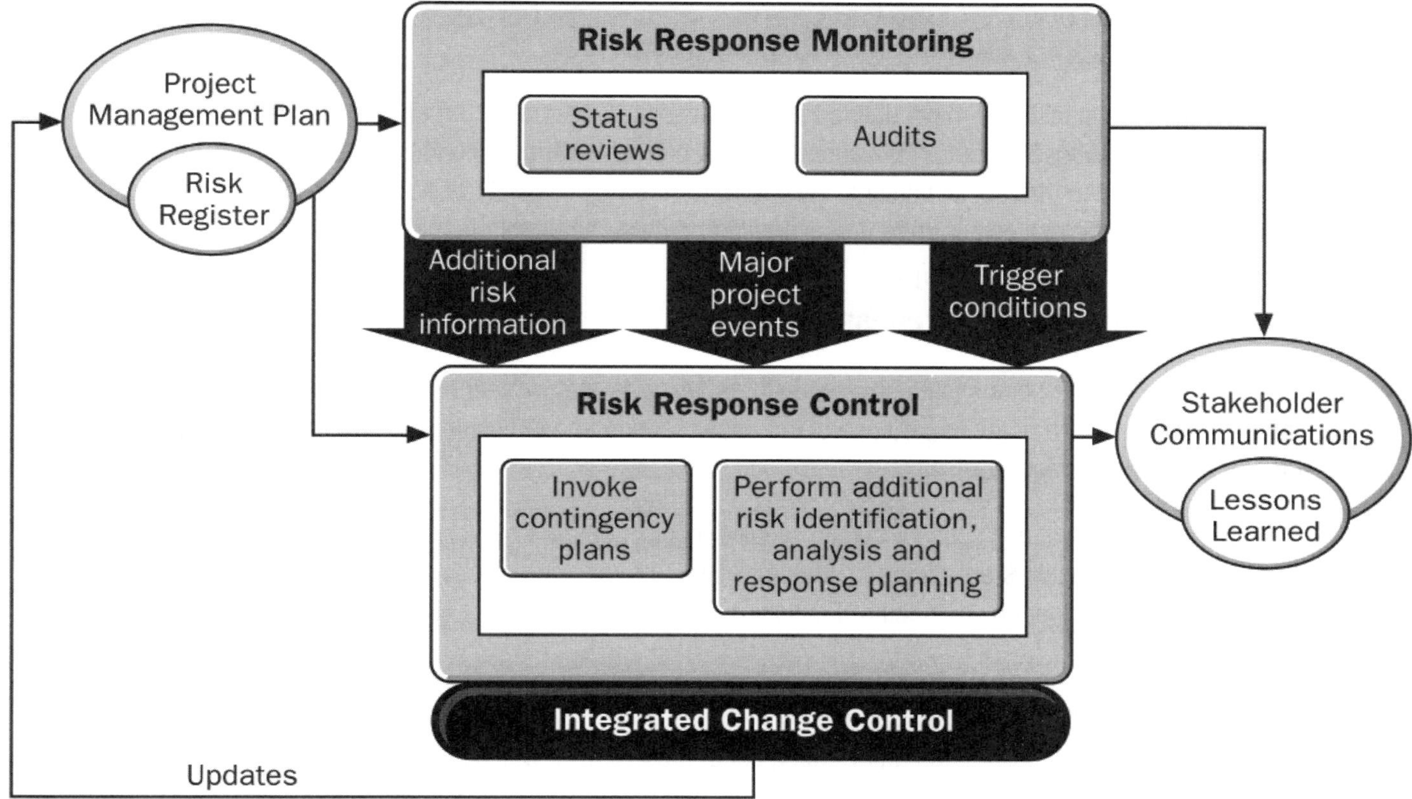

Figure 9-1. Schematic Representation of the Monitor and Control Risks Process

9.2 Critical Success Factors for the Monitor and Control Risks Process

Critical success factors relate to maintaining risk awareness throughout the project and include the characteristics and capabilities detailed in Sections 9.2.1 through 9.2.3.

9.2.1 Integrate Risk Monitoring and Control with Project Monitoring and Control

From the start, the project management plan should include the actions required to monitor and control project risk. This should be set up early in the project planning cycle, and then adjusted in view of the risk response planning decisions adding, for example, the actions associated with monitoring specific conditions or metrics. Once risk response planning has been carried out, the project schedule should include all of the agreed-upon, response-related actions so that they can be carried out as a normal part of project execution and tracked accordingly.

9.2.2 Continuously Monitor Risk Trigger Conditions

Risk response planning will have defined a set of actions to be carried out as part of the project schedule as well as actions whose execution is dependent on a predefined trigger condition. Checking for specifically defined risks that may trigger conditional responses is the responsibility of the risk action owner, in close collaboration with the risk owner under the overall authority of the project manager.

9.2.3 Maintain Risk Awareness

Risk management reports should be a regular item on every status meeting agenda to ensure that all team members remain aware of the importance of risk management and to ensure that it is fully integrated into all of the project management decisions.

The project's senior-level sponsor should require regular reports on the risks and the planned responses to ensure that stakeholders are aware of the importance of keeping a focus on risk. Sponsor feedback also motivates the project team by demonstrating senior-level interest in Project Risk Management.

Stakeholders' perception of the effectiveness of risk management is conditioned in part by the way in which risks are handled as they occur, and by the number or characteristics of such events. It is therefore crucial, whenever a risk occurs, that information about the event, as well as the progress and effectiveness of the responses, be communicated at regular intervals and in an honest manner adapted to the needs of each stakeholder. This should be supported by a well-executed communications plan.

9.3 Tools and Techniques for the Monitor and Control Risks Process

In addition to standard project management monitoring and control capabilities, risk monitoring and controlling requires a focus on the tools which will support its key success factors for tracking overall risk as well as individual risks.

9.3.1 Managing Contingency Reserves

Reserves may have been allocated separately to cover time-related and cost-related risks. Techniques are required that allow the project manager to assess at any point in the project whether these provide the required level of confidence in the success of the project.

Tools for managing time buffers should be closely integrated into the project's scheduling techniques, whereas those for managing cost should be compatible with the financial practices. Tools are required to identify trends and forecast future outcomes to determine whether the reserves will remain sufficient. Tools are also required for tracking progress and spending in a consolidated manner.

9.3.2 Tracking Trigger Conditions

Trigger conditions and the corresponding metrics are defined during the Plan Risk Responses process. Tools are required to evaluate and track these conditions against the project baseline or specified thresholds, based on actual status. They can be chosen to provide information on risks related to the deliverables, such as performance, as well as on project-related features, such as time and cost.

9.3.3 Tracking Overall Risk

Tools are required in order to determine, as the project progresses, whether the responses are having the expected effect on the project's overall level of risk.

9.3.4 Tracking Compliance

In order to monitor the quality of the execution of the risk-related plans and processes, a set of quality metrics such as degree of variation from the baseline, should be tracked and recorded. These metrics will normally have been defined in the risk management plan.

9.4 Documenting the Results of the Monitor and Control Risks Process

The final control action of risk monitoring and controlling is to record actual data for future use. This includes all of the relevant information relating to risk management from start to finish of the project. The definition of what this information must include, as well as the storage mechanism, should have been previously specified in the risk management plan.

The goal is to ensure that the significant risk management information is recorded to provide concrete data to the lessons learned process for inclusion in a lessons learned document, report, or other communication vehicle. Typical information includes the following:

- For each identified risk or type of risk, whether it occurred, and, if so, when and how often. All relevant data should be recorded: impact, effectiveness of detection and of response, and any unplanned, additional actions that were carried out.
- Effectiveness of avoidance or exploitation actions.
- Effectiveness of transfer and sharing actions.
- Unexpected or undocumented risks which occurred and data about them.
- Effectiveness of risk mitigation and enhancement actions.
- Occurrence of accepted threats or opportunities.

Consolidated information should be provided on the level of effort expended. Costs and benefits to the project of risk management activities should also be provided.

This information will need to be archived and indexed in a manner that will facilitate retrieval for easy review during the project, at closure, and for future projects, when the need arises.

APPENDIX A

GUIDELINES FOR A PMI PRACTICE STANDARD

A.1 Introduction

A PMI practice standard is characterized as follows:

- Each practice standard provides guidelines on the mechanics (e.g., nuts and bolts, basics, fundamentals, step-by-step usage guide, how it operates, how to do it) of some significant process (input, tool, technique, or output) that is relevant to a project manager.
- A practice standard does not necessarily mirror the life-cycle phases of many projects; however, an individual practice standard may be applicable to the completion of one or more phases within a project.
- A practice standard does not necessarily mirror the Knowledge Areas within *A Guide to the Project Management Body of Knowledge* (*PMBOK® Guide*–Fourth Edition), although an individual practice standard will provide sufficient detail and background for one or more of the inputs, tools and techniques, and/or outputs. Therefore, practice standards are not required to use the name of any Knowledge Area.
- Each practice standard should include information on what the significant process is and does, why it is significant, how to perform it, when it should be performed, and, if necessary for further clarification, who should perform it.
- Each practice standard should include information that is accepted and applicable for most projects most of the time within the project management community. Processes that are generally restricted or applicable to one industry, country, or companion profession (i.e., an *application area*) may be included as an appendix for informational purposes, rather than as part of the practice standard. With strong support and evidence, an application area-specific process may be considered as an extension practice standard, in the same manner as extensions to the *PMBOK® Guide*–Fourth Edition are considered.
- Each practice standard will benefit from the inclusion of examples and templates. It is best when an example or template includes a discussion of its strengths and weaknesses. A background description may be necessary to put this discussion in the appropriate context. The examples should be aligned with the relevant information in the standard or its appendix and placed in proximity to that information.
- All practice standards shall be written in the same general style and format.
- Each practice standard project will be aligned with or reference other practice standards, as needed.
- Each practice standard will be consistent with the *PMBOK® Guide*–Fourth Edition.
- Each practice standard is intended to be more prescriptive than the *PMBOK® Guide*–Fourth Edition.

APPENDIX B

EVOLUTION OF PMI'S *PRACTICE STANDARD FOR PROJECT RISK MANAGEMENT*

B.1 Pre-Project

In early 2005, PMI began exploration for developing the first Practice Standard for Project Risk Management. Focus would be placed on single project risk management for a single project rather than including programs or portfolios of projects, with close coupling to the Project Risk Management section of *A Guide to the Project Management Body of Knowledge (PMBOK® Guide)* – Third Edition. By April 20, 2006, the PMI Standards Members Advisory Group (MAG) approved the following final charter for the standard, with Cynthia A. Berg, PMP, as the Project Manager, and Dr. David Hulett as the Deputy Project Manager. The charter included the following characteristics for the standard:

- Provides information on Project Risk Management that includes information that is clear, complete, relevant, and generally recognized as good practice on most projects most of the time.
- Is consistent with the *PMBOK® Guide* – Third Edition, expanding but not contradicting, the concepts and techniques related to Project Risk Management, and keeps within the limits and practices of Project Risk Management as described within Chapter 11 of the *PMBOK® Guide*– Third Edition.
- Has been reviewed and updated by the Practice Standard for Project Risk Management Project Team.
- Is written for project management practitioners and other stakeholders of the project management profession.
- Describes the processes that are unique to Project Risk Management.
- Includes in an appendix, examples and templates of specific Project Risk Management processes, tools, and/or techniques addressed in the practice standard, with discussions of their strengths and weaknesses, including background descriptions that put the relative strengths and weaknesses into context.
- Uses the *PMBOK® Guide* – Third Edition Glossary as the starting point of its glossary, and does not contain contradictions.
- Uses a glossary term in the text without definition or additional explanation.
- Is aligned with and does not contradict other PMI standards.
- Follows the PMI Style Guide, is written in North American English, translatable to PMI official languages, and is sensitive to cultural issues.

- Can be approved as a PMI standard, which means that in addition to the content being acceptable, the process for selecting team members and soliciting and responding to comments on the product must be open and inclusive.

B.2 Preliminary Work

In recognition that risk management is not practiced well on many projects, the project team set out to identify practices that are viewed as best practices, as those are understood, and applied in most successfully managed projects most of the time.

The project core team was initially formed in the fall of 2005 and consisted of; Dr. David Hillson PMP, Kik Piney, and Kris Persun.

B.3 Scope Changes

During the time the project was chartered, the *PMBOK® Guide* – Fourth Edition was commissioned. As a result, the charter of the Practice Standard for Project Risk Management was expanded to be consistent and non-contradictory with that standard.

B.4 Exposure and Consensus

The standard was submitted as an exposure draft in the winter of 2007, and exposed on 23 March 2008. There were 849 comments. The team's comment acceptance rate (comments accepted outright, and accepted with modifications) was 57%. The PMI Standards Manager submitted the resultant final draft, with the concurrence of the PMI Standards Program MAG, to the PMI Standards Program Consensus Body for official ballot on 27 March 2009. Twenty-eight members of the PMI Standards Program Consensus Body agreed to participate in the ballot of the *Practice Standard for Project Risk Management.* Those not participating included the PM and Deputy PM for this standard because their participation was considered a conflict of interest. The balloting period was closed on 25 April 2009 with 23 ballots returned. Consensus Body voting results were as follows: 22 affirmative and 1 affirmative with comment. The affirmative with comment pertained to future revisions of the standard and possible improvements to the comment adjudication process.

APPENDIX C

CONTRIBUTORS AND REVIEWERS OF THE *PRACTICE STANDARD FOR PROJECT RISK MANAGEMENT*

This appendix lists, alphabetically within groupings, those individuals who have contributed to the development and production of the *Practice Standard for Project Risk Management.* No simple list or even multiple lists can adequately convey all the contributions of those who have volunteered to develop the *Practice Standard for Project Risk Management.*

The Project Management Institute is grateful to all of these individuals for their support and acknowledges their contributions to the project management profession.

C.1 *Practice Standard for Project Risk Management* Project Core Team

The following individuals served as members, were contributors of text or concepts, and served as leaders within the Project Core Team (PCT):

Cynthia Ann Berg, PhD, PMP Project Manager
David T. Hulett, PhD, Deputy Project Manager
Dr. David Hillson FRSA, FIRM
Kristine Persun, MA, PMP
Crispin "Kik" Piney, BSc, PMP
Kristin L. Vitello, Standards Project Specialist
Nan Wolfslayer, AStd, Standards Compliance Specialist

C.2 Significant Contributors

In addition to the members of the Project Core Team and the Sub-Team Leaders, the following individuals provided significant input or concepts:

Jeannette Horne

C.3 *Practice Standard for Project Risk Management* Team Members

In addition to those listed above, the following individuals participated on the *Practice Standard for Project Risk Management* Project Team.

Ahmad Khairiri Abdul Ghani, PE, MBA
Archie Addo, PMP, PhD
Priumvada Agarwal, PMP
Upinder Aggarwal, PMP
Asif M Ahmad, PMP
Amr Nabil Ahmed, PMP, MSc
Jose Correia Alberto, MEng, CITP
Salvador Alvarez, PMP
Chukwudi Anakudo, PMP
Ananthalakshmi Anbuselvan
Jagathnarayanan Angyan, FIE, CE
Rodrigo Ariza
Pedro Carlos Auler
Michael Avery
Sai Swaminathan Baba Subramanyan, BE, PMP
Teddy Alton Barnes
Gail Ellen Bartz
David Benfell
Paul S. Bennett
Douglas A. Berry, PMP
Mamoun Besaiso, CE
Timothy Birus
Dave M. Bond
Kiron Bondale
Blaine W. Boxwell, MBA, PMP
Carlos Eduardo M. F. Braga, PMP
Valerie Claire Brasse, PMP
Joan Browne, BSc, PMP
Adrian Busch, PMP, MBA
John J. Byrne, DBA, PMP
C. S. Rajan, PMP
Eduardo Cadena
Franco Caron
William G. Chadick, DM, PMP
Souray Chakraborty
Harshavardhan Chakravarti, BS
Shanthi Chandrasekar
Noman Zafar Chaudry, PE, PMP
Vijay Chauhan, MBA, PMP
Subrahmanyam Chinta, VN, PMP
Carolyn Chomik
Joan F. Church
Glenda Clark
Lorri Cline, MBA, PMP
John D. Corless, PhD
Anthony R. Corridore, PMP
Coughlin, Philip
Nancy A Cygan, MS, PMP
Marco Aurélio Danelon, PMP
Karel de Bakker, MA, PMP
Thijs De Jong
Alfredo Del Cano
Peter B. de Zouza Mello, SPS, PMP
Cheryl L. Dennis
Raveesh Dewan, PMP, MBA
Ricardo Jose do Rego Barros, PMP
John David Driessnack
Matt Dubois
Jason Eddinger, PMP
Maliha Elahi, MSc, PMP
Norman Epstein, PMP, MBA
Joel Erickson
Rodrigo Fernandes Espirito Santo
Giovanni Fanduiz
Geneviève Faragó, PMP
Mario Fiallo Carranco
Leslie Fiedler
Eduardo Fleischer

Kirby Fortenberry, PMP
Michelle L. Franklin, PMP
Andrew Fry, CMA, PMP
Nélio Gaspar, MSc, PMP
Silvio Hernan Giraldo, PMP, CBCP
Vivek Goel, PMP
Serge Goncharov, PMP, PgMP
Priyesh Gopalakrishnan
Steve Grunewald
Sanjay Gupta, PMP
Heidi Ann Hahn, PhD, PMP
Robert W. Harding, PMP
Chandrashekar Hassan
David A. Haugh, PMP
Arnold A. Hill, PMP
George Hopman, PhD, PE
John Humphrey
George Jackelen
Dhanojkumar Jadhav
Stephen Michael Johns
Valeri Jonas, BA (Honours), Oxon
Krishna Kallapur, PMP
Mariya Kehoe
Amir Ahmed Kheir
Konstantinos Kirytopoulos, PhD, PMP
Alejandro Kowiendl
Jeyakumar Krishamoorthy
Polisetty Veera Subrahmanya Kumar, CISSP, CISA
Vijaya Kurada
David Larson
Henry Lie
Bernard Lindekens
Vasantha R Manda, PMP, CISSP
Rivalino Matias Jr., PhD, MSc
JME Maxwell MBA, PMP
Traci L. McIntosh, PMP
Concepcion Merino

Lynn Francis
Tracy Fritz
Kamlesh Gandhi, PMP, PQs
Tina Gilrein, PMP, MPM
Vikram Godboley
Francisco Gomez
Ronald R.Goodwin, PMP
Robert Grant
Denise M. Guerin
Cristine Gusmão, PhD
Laurie Hall
Balasubramaniam Hari Gopal, FCA, PMP
Henry Hattenrath
John Hendricks, MS, PMP
Rosemarie A. Hilt, MBA, PMP
Sean Hugo
Walter Hussey, PMP
Ramona Jackson
Ayo Jemiri, MS, PMP
Kenneth E. Johnson, MBA, PMP
Roy Joslin
Rita Kaul
Rameshchandra B. Ketharaju
Behrad Kiafar
Ilkka Koskinen, MSc, PMP
R.V. Krishna, MBA, CAPM
Lars Kruse
Sasi Kumar, PMP
Elise Labre
Wei Lee, PMP
Guilherme Pereira Lima, PMP
Renato Lourenço da Silva, MBA, PMP
Edmond Matevosian, PE, PMP
Peña Torres Nestor Mauricio, PMP
Alvis McGinty
Ramesh Menon
Philip Mileham

Waqar Ahmed Mirza
Siddique Mohammed
Sergio Monaco, MCTS
Flavio Montenegro, PMP
Linda L. Morgan, MSIS, PMP
Tania Morris MPM, PMP
Mark A. Munster PMP, CISA
Carlo Muzzarelli
Rob Nelson, PMP
Ann Nguyen, PMP
Jillian O'Connell, MBA, PMP
Armin Oppitz, PMP
Abhimanyu Parasher, MBA, PMP
Scott Patton
Chris Payne, PMP
Alexandre Perali
Lavinia Petcu, CAPM
Krista Lynn Pizzurro
Carl Pro
Sridhar R Pydah, MS, PMP
Stephen F. Randolph, PMBA PMP
Caroline Robison, PMP
Edward Rowe
Joseph Sabatini
Salem Mahaboob Saliha Sherriff, MBA, PMP
Rudolf Schenker
Bill Schneider
Ravi Shanker, MBA, PMP
Jeff Shore
Maria Isabel Silva Sumano, MBA, PMP
Vivek Sivakumar, CAPM
Shaun Smith
Mauro Sotille, PMP
Tournis Stamatis, PhD PMP
Roeland Stellingwerff
Prasanna V Sugavanam, PMP
Matthias Svane, MSc, PMP
Shipra Mitra
Guillermo Molina Leon
Elizabeth Mejia Montanez
Mohammad Moradi
Rick A. Morris, MPM, PMP
Saradhi Motamarri, MTech, PMP
Ronan J. Murphy, CEng, MBA
Linda Nedney, PMP
Vaman G. Nene
Naema Nunnery
Daryl K. Ono
Daniel Pacholski, PMP
David M. Patrick
Mridul Paul
Sameer K Penakalapati, ME, PMP
Sharon D. Perez-Suarez
Bruce Petro, PMP
Roberto Pons, PMP
Julie R. Purcell, PMP, MCSE
Vijaya Raman, PMP
Jennifer Read, PMP, CMC
Fabiano Rollim, PMP, PgMP
Don Ruchkall
Fawzia Salahuddin MCS, PMP
Sivakumar Sanyasi
Marcio Schmidt, PMP
Michael J. Scott, PMP
Viresh C Shah, MBA, PMP
Evandro Silva
Michael D. Simants
Kathy J. Slater, PMP
Linda E. Solorzano, BS, PMP
Mandayam Sriram, Meng, PMP
Fred Stein
Jim Stewart, PMP
Ramakrishnan Sundararaman
Amin Tabatabayi, MBA, PMP

Venerando Tangco, PMP, CSM
Patel Tejesh, PMP
Jacqueline Teo
Gangesh Thakur, CPIM, PMP
Ing. Biagio Tramontana, PMP
Ruth H. Vandegrift
Christoph Verschuere, Ir, PMP, CISM
Yiannis Vithynos, PMP, MSc
Paul Waits Jr., PMP, CPM
Nancy Watanabe
Lisa L. Winchester, PMP
James Yang, PMP, MBA
Xiaojun Zhou
Suresh Kumar Tata, PMP, ACS
Sarma Tekumalla, PMP, MBA
Michelle Tessier
Vadivelu Thanicachalam
Subhash B. Tuladhar, PMP
Sri Pavan Vardan Vemu
Marianne Viegas
Steve Waddell
Kuan-Hsun Wang, PMP
James Wattnem
Karen L. Woodruff, RN CFNP, PMP
Luay M. Zakaria, PMP

C.4 Final Exposure Draft Reviewers and Contributors

In addition to team members, the following individuals provided recommendations for improving the Exposure Draft of the *Practice Standard for Project Risk Management*:

Marcos Abreu
José R. Alcalá G., PMP
Mohd Al-Kuwari
Ondiappan Arivazhagan "Ari", PMP, PMI-RMP
Randall Ash, PMP
Imad Babbili
Ernest Baker, PMP
Jerry Ball, PMP
Eng. Dimah M. Barakat, PMP, PMI-RMP
Suvransu Basu, BE
Susanne Bode
David J. Boschma PMP B.E.
Sergio A. Calvo Abarca, PMP
Marlene Carnevali
Bruce C. Chadbourne, PMP, PgMP
Steve Charters MAPM MSc
Tomio Chiba, PMP
Patricia Cohen
Wendra Collet, MPM
Billa S. Dahaby, MS, ISSI
Gwendolyn Darby
Anirban Das, M.Tech, PMP
Terrell G. Dorn, PE
Peggy Drew, MBA, PMP
Norberto Figuerola, PMP
Robert A. Dudley, PMP, PMI-SP
Scott D. Freauf, PMP, IPMA-D
Mark Gabel, MSCE, PE
Oliver D. Gildersleeve, Jr., PMP, MCTS
Kurt J. Harris, PMP
Jame Healy
Walter Hekala, CQA, PMP
Shirley Hinton, PMP
Felicia Elizabeth Hong, PMP, MBA
Manuel Huerta
Kristian Hurt
Christoph Werner Jacobi
Ashok Jain, PMP, ITIL

Syed Asad Jawed C.C.E
Ramesh D. Kandadai, member RSIG
Kenneth P. Katz PMP
Rameshchandra Ketharaju
Gene G. Kuki, PMP
Abhilash T. Kuzhikat, PMP, ITIL
Peter Lierni
Christopher E. Maddox, PMP
Anthony Mampilly, PMP, COP
Srinivas Mandgi, PMP, SAP HR
Ammar W. Mango, PgMP, PMP
Larry Marks
Andrew McGlade, PMP
Patrick K. Morrow, PMP
Rajesh Musaliyath
Eric M. Myers, PMP
Mustapha NAFAÂ, MPM, PMP
Patrick O'Farrell, PMP, MBA
Lambert I. Ofoegbu, PMP, PMI-RMP
Kazuhiko Okubo, PMP, PE
Karthikeyan Ovuraj
Nancy Perosio, PMP
Rafael Piña Quintal
Dirk Pons
Carl L. Pritchard, PMP, PMI-RMP
Javier Pumar, PMP
Polisetty Veera Subrahmanya Kumar, PMP, PMI-RMP
Chandrasekar Ramakrishnan PMP, CSQA
Ivan D. Ramirez R., PMP
Alexander Revin, PMP
Pedro C. Ribeiro, MBA, PMP
Bruce P. Robison
Sadegh Roozbehi
Tarun Kumar Roy
Balaji Selvaraju
Hilary Shreter, MBA, PMP
Fay Simcock MSc, PMP
Rebecca Spohn, PMP, CQE
Pranay Srivastava, PMP, CSM
Joyce Statz, PhD, PMP
Massimo Torre, PhD, PMP
Fredrick G. Trussell, PMP
Frederick Trussell
Kevin R. Wegryn, PMP, CPM
William. E. Wencel, PMP
Alexey D. Zimin, PME

C.5 PMI Standards Member Advisory Group (MAG)

The following individuals served as members of the PMI Standards Member Advisory Group (MAG) during development of the *Practice Standard for Project Risk Management*:

Julia M. Bednar, PMP
Douglas Clark
Carol Holliday, MA, PMP
Asbjørn Rolstadås, PhD, Ing
Paul E. Shaltry, PMP
David Violette, MPM, PMP
Chris Cartwright, MPM, PMP
Terry Cooke-Davies, PhD FCMI
Deborah O'Bray, CIM (Hons)
David W. Ross, PMP, PgMP
Cynthia Stackpole, MBA, PMP
John Zlockie, MBA, PMP

C.6 Staff Contributors

Special mention is due to the following employees of PMI:

Steven L. Fahrenkrog, PMP, VP Regional Development

Amanda Freitick, Standards Program Administrator

Ruth Anne Guerrero, MBA, PMP, Former Standards Manager

Donn Greenberg, Manager, Publications

Roberta Storer, Product Editor

Barbara Walsh, CAPM, Publications Planner

APPENDIX D

TOOLS, TECHNIQUES AND TEMPLATES FOR PROJECT RISK MANAGEMENT

Many tools and techniques have been developed and are in widespread use to support the Project Risk Management processes. The most commonly used of these are listed in the following tables along with their strengths, weaknesses, and critical success factors. Where a technique can be used in more than one Project Risk Management process, it is described in detail in the section associated with the main process that it supports, and referred to as necessary for other processes to which it can be of use. Examples and templates shown after each table provide illustrations of the most common and good practice uses of these tools and techniques. This information is not intended to explain the tools and techniques but to list them with certain important characteristics. Those who are interested in learning more are encouraged to seek other sources such as handbooks, textbooks, or courses in project risk management.

D.1 Techniques, Examples and Templates for Risk Management Planning (Chapter 4)

Plan Risk Management defines the approach to be followed for managing the risks throughout the lifespan of the corresponding project.

D.1.1 Techniques

An example of an approach is given in Table D1.

Table D1. Example of Plan Risk Management Approach

Technique	Strengths	Weaknesses	CSFs for Effective Application
Planning Meetings and Analysis	• Involvement of core team members	• Depends on experience of participants	• Prior risk management plan templates • Prior stakeholder analysis • Existing organizational guidelines for risk management

D.1.1.1 The Risk Management Plan – Purpose and Typical Content

Depending on the size and complexity of the project, some or all of the following elements will be present in a risk management plan.

- **Introduction**
- Project Description
    - Project objectives
    - External dependencies
    - Stakeholder analysis
- Risk Management Scope and Objectives
    - Variance thresholds
    - Prioritization of project objectives
    - Thresholds, weights and other parameters
        - Definition of criteria for "unacceptable threats" and "un-missable opportunities"
        - Impact scales, probability scales, PxI matrices, weighting of project objectives, prioritization and selection criteria, degree of confidence required for overall risk (e.g., 80th percentile) from quantitative risk analysis
- Risk Management Methodology
    - Relationship with the organizational environment
    - Risk management activities
        - Link to the project management methodology
        - Relationship with other project management processes
    - Risk taxonomy/risk breakdown structure (either generic or project-specific)
    - Format of a fully defined risk statement description ("metalanguage")
    - Key deliverables
- Risk Management Organization
    - Roles, responsibilities and levels of authority for risk management
        - Rules of escalation
    - Budgeting for risk management activities added to the project budget
        - Adapted to the complexity and sensitivity of the project
    - Scheduling of risk management activities in the project schedule, i.e. when certain actions or reviews need to be carried out (frequency, life cycle related, etc.)

    - Reporting
        - Governance-related rules of reporting and disclosure
- Use of Tools
    - Tool name, description, usage
    - Structure of the risk database
        - Requirements in terms of system resources
- Communications Planning
    - Documents, usage, rules for distribution (frequency, audience, etc.)
    - Document templates
        - Risk register
        - Risk status reports

D.1.1.2 Templates Relevant to Risk Management Planning

The risk management plan should provide a number of templates for use by the other processes. These may include:

- Formal structure for a risk statement
    - An example is given below
- Means of categorizing risks, for example a risk breakdown structure
    - An example is given in the Identify Risks section of this appendix
- Definitions, by project objective, of probability and impact scales
    - An example is given in the Perform Qualitative Risk Analysis section of this appendix
- Risk prioritization and selection guidelines
    - These guidelines may be used in Perform Qualitative Risk Analysis and in Perform Quantitative Risk Analysis as well as in Plan Risk Response Planning. An example is given below.
- Status report templates
- Typical agenda for status meetings

D.1.1.3 Risk Statement "Metalanguage"

In order for all risks to be clearly defined, a standard structure for the way in which the risk is described should be specified and applied. A typical such statement is:

"Because of <one or more causes>, <risk> might occur, which would lead to <one or more effects>".

D.1.1.4 Risk Prioritization and Selection Guidelines

The selection and prioritization of risks must be linked to the project objectives. The risk management plan will define the relative importance to be assigned to these objectives (e.g. reliability takes precedence over time, etc.): this may be in the form of numerical "weights" that can be applied to create a single weighted sum over all objectives for each risk. Any other features that may affect the urgency of dealing with a risk should also be specified (e.g. one linked to a resource that will soon disappear should be given greater urgency).

D.2 Techniques, Examples and Templates for Identify Risks (Chapter 5)

Identify Risks is carried out in order to develop a comprehensive list of all knowable uncertainties that could have an effect on the project's objectives.

Table D2. Identify Risks

Technique	Strengths	Weaknesses	CSFs for Effective Application
Assumptions & Constraints Analysis	• Simple structured approach • Can be based on assumptions & constraints already listed in project charter • Generates project-specific risks	• Implicit/hidden assumptions or constraints are often missed	• Requires a comprehensive list of assumptions & constraints
Brainstorming	• Allows all participants to speak their mind and contribute to the discussion • Can involve all key stakeholders • Creative generation of ideas	• Requires attendance of key stakeholders at a workshop, therefore can be difficult to arrange and expensive • Prone to Groupthink and other group dynamics • May produce biased results if dominated by a strong person (often management) • Often not well facilitated • Generates non-risks and duplicates, requires filtering	• Attendance of representative group of stakeholders • Commitment to honesty • Preparation • Good facilitation • Use of structure (e.g. categories or RBS)
Cause and Effect (Ishikawa) Diagrams	• Visual representation of project promotes structured thinking	• Diagram can quickly become over-complex	• Effective selection of critical impacts (e.g. by use of sensitivity analysis)

Table D2. Identify Risks *(continued)*

Technique	Strengths	Weaknesses	CSFs for Effective Application
Check Lists	• Captures previous experience • Presents detailed list of risks	• Check list can grow to become unwieldy • Risks not on the list will be missed • Often only includes threats, misses opportunities	• Regular maintenance is required • Use of structure can assist (e.g. RBS)
Delphi Technique	• Captures input from technical experts • Removes sources of bias	• Limited to technical risks • Dependent on actual expertise of experts • May take longer time than available due to iterations of the experts' inputs	• Effective facilitation • Careful selection of experts • Clear definition of scope
Document review	• Exposes detailed project-specific risks • Requires no specialist tools	• Limited to risks contained in project documentation	• Understanding of relevance of prior experience
FMEA/Fault Tree Analysis → *see Chapter 7*	• Structured approach, well understood by engineers • Produces an estimate of overall reliability using quantitative tools • Good tool support	• Focuses on threats, not so useful for opportunities • Requires expert tools not generally available to those except experts	• Detailed description of the area being assessed • Statistically accurate data on fault probabilities for many events
Force Field Analysis	• Creates deep understanding of factors that affect project objectives	• Time-consuming and complex technique • Usually only applied to a single objective, so does not provide whole-project view	• Prioritized objectives
Industry knowledge base	• Captures previous experience • Allows benchmarking against external organisations	• Limited to what has previously happened • Excludes project-specific risks	• Access to relevant information

(continued)

Table D2. Identify Risks *(continued)*

Technique	Strengths	Weaknesses	CSFs for Effective Application
Influence diagrams	• Exposes key risk drivers • Can generate counter-intuitive insights not available through other techniques	• Requires disciplined thinking • Not always easy to determine appropriate structure	• Identify key areas to address
Interviews	• Addresses risks in detail • Generates engagement of stakeholders	• Time consuming • Raises non-risks, concerns, issues, worries etc, so requires filtering	• Good interviewing and questioning skills • Environment of trust, openness, confidentiality • Preparation • Open relationship between interviewer and interviewee
Nominal Group Technique	• Encourages and allows all participants to contribute • Allows for different levels of competence in common language • To a large extent, auto-documenting • Provides ideal base for affinity diagramming (grouping by risk categories for use in the Risk Breakdown Structure and Root Cause Analysis)	• Can lead to frustration in dominant members who feel it is moving slowly	• Good briefing of all participants in the technique • Strict facilitation
Post-project reviews/ Lessons Learned/ Historical Information → *see Chapter 6*	• Leverages previous experience • Prevents making the same mistakes or missing the same opportunities twice • Enhances the Organizational Process Assets	• Limited to those risks that have occurred previously • Information is frequently incomplete: details of past risks may not include details of successful resolution; ineffective strategies are rarely documented.	• Well structured project lessons learned database • Participation of previous project team members (ideally including the project manager)
Prompt Lists	• Ensures coverage of all types of risk • Stimulates creativity	• Topics can be too high level	• Choice of list relevant to the project and its environment

Table D2. Identify Risks *(continued)*

Technique	Strengths	Weaknesses	CSFs for Effective Application
Questionnaire	• Encourages broad thinking to identify risks	• Success depends on the quality of the questions • Limited to the topics covered by the questions • Can be a simple reformatting of a checklist	• Clear and unambiguous questions • Detailed briefing of respondents
Risk Breakdown Structure (RBS)	• Offers a framework for other risk identification techniques such as brainstorming • Ensures coverage of all types of risk • Tests for blind spots or omissions	• None	• Requires a comprehensive RBS, often tailored to the project
Root-Cause Analysis → *see Chapter 6*	• Allows identification of additional, dependent risks • Allows the organization to identify risks that may be related because of their common root causes. • Basis for development of pre-emptive and comprehensive responses • Can serve to reduce apparent complexity	• Most risk management techniques are organized by individual risk. This organization is not conducive to identifying the root causes • Can oversimplify and hide existence of other potential causes • There may be no valid strategy available for addressing the root cause once it has been identified.	• Ability to identify if a risk is an outcome of a more fundamental cause • Willingness by management to accept and address the root cause rather than adopting partial workarounds
SWOT Analysis	• Ensures equal focus on both threats and opportunities • Offers a structured approach to identify threats and opportunities • Focus on internal (organizational strengths and weaknesses) and external (opportunities and threats)	• Focuses on internally generated risks arising from organizational strengths and weaknesses, excludes external risks • Tends to produce high-level generic risks, not project-specific	• Good facilitation • Strict adherence to the technique, to avoid confusing the four SWOT perspectives (i.e. between Strengths and Opportunities, or between Weaknesses and Threats)

(continued)

Table D2. Identify Risks *(continued)*

Technique	Strengths	Weaknesses	CSFs for Effective Application
System Dynamics → *see Chapter 715*	• Exposes unexpected inter-relations between project elements (feedback and feed-forward loops) • Can generate counter-intuitive insights not available through other techniques • Produces overall impacts of all included events and risks	• Requires specialized software and expertise to build models • Focuses on impacts but difficult to include the concept of probability	• Understanding of feedback • Competence in applying tools and understanding their output • Quality of the system model • Accuracy of input data collected for the specific project
WBS Review	• Ensures all elements of the project scope are considered • Provides for risks related to different levels of detail (from high-level to those related to individual work packages)	• Excludes external risks or those not specifically related to WBS elements	• Good WBS

D.2.1 Techniques

Examples of techniques are given in D.2.1.1 through D.2.1.15.

D.2.1.1 Assumptions and Constraints Analysis

This technique requires three steps:

1. List assumptions and constraints for the project
2. Test assumptions and constraints by asking two questions:
   a. Could the assumption/constraint be false?
   b. If it were false, would one or more project objectives be affected (positively or negatively)?
3. Where both questions are answered "Yes", generate a risk, for example in the form: <Assumption/constraint> may prove false, leading to <effect on objective(s)>.

The results can be documented in table form, as shown in Figure D1.

Assumption or Constraint	Could this assumption/constraint prove false? (Y/N)	If false would it affect project? (Y/N)	Convert to a risk?

Figure D1. Example of a Constraint Analysis with Fields for Description and Analysis Results

D.2.1.2 Brainstorming

Brainstorming is commonly used in a facilitated risk identification workshop to identify risks. The standard rules of brainstorming are often modified when the technique is applied to risk identification. For example it is common to structure the risk identification brainstorm using risk categories or a risk breakdown structure. Some evaluation of proposed risks is often included in a risk identification brainstorm to remove non-risks. It is important to ensure active participation of relevant stakeholders in a risk identification brainstorm, and for the facilitator to manage group dynamics carefully. No templates or examples are presented in this appendix.

D.2.1.3 Cause and Effect (Ishikawa) Diagrams

This technique presents in diagrammatic form the causes which contribute to a given outcome. Each main cause can be split further into sub-causes. To use this technique for risk identification the outcome should be stated as an effect on a project objective, i.e. the impact of a risk. The diagram then identifies risks as those uncertain events which could result in occurrence of the impact. Care needs to be taken when using this technique for risk identification to distinguish between risks (uncertain causes of the impact) and issues (certain causes of the impact). An example cause and effect (Ishikawa) diagram is shown below: the risk (effect) to be analyzed is "staff leaving the project"; the main causes are Environment, Ambition, Career Prospects, Satisfaction, Remuneration.

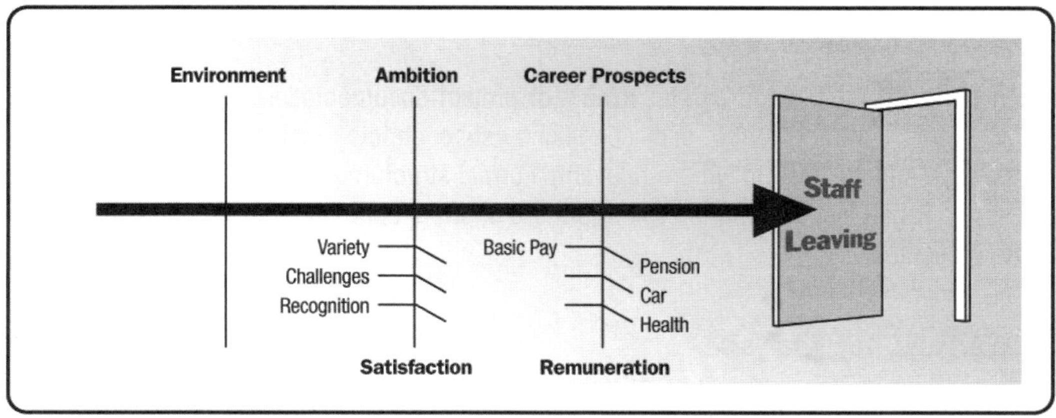

Figure D2. Example of a Cause and Effect or Ishikawa Diagram for Staff Leaving

D.2.1.4 Checklists

Checklists are compiled to capture previous project experience and allow it to be used for subsequent similar projects. It is possible to structure the risk identification checklist around a risk breakdown structure, as shown in the partial example below. It is useful to present the checklist as a set of risks, each of which is considered in turn to determine whether it might be relevant to the project under consideration. Risk identification checklists should include both threats and opportunities.

RISK CATEGORY	SUBCATEGORY	EXAMPLE RISKS	Could this risk affect our project? **Yes, No Don't know, Not applicable**
1. TECHNICAL RISK	1.1 Scope definition	Scope changes may arise during project.	
		Redundant scope may be discovered.	
		Etc...	
	1.2 Technical interfaces	Etc...	

Figure D3. Example (Fragment) of a Checklist with Typical Structure of Category, Subcategory, Specific Risks and Effect

D.2.1.5 Delphi Technique

The Delphi technique uses a facilitated anonymous polling of subject matter experts to identify risks in their area of expertise. The facilitator gathers the experts' initial responses and circulates them without attribution to the group, who may revise their contributions based on those of others. The process often generates a consensus of the experts in a few iterations. No templates or examples are presented.

D.2.1.6 Document Review

Risks can be identified through careful review of project documentation, including the project charter, statement of work, contract terms and conditions, subcontracts, technical specifications, regulatory requirements, legal stipulations etc (where relevant). Formal structured methods of document review can be used (such as the Fagan Inspection Process), or a more informal approach may be adopted. No templates or examples are presented.

D.2.1.7 FMEA/Fault Tree Analysis

Failure Modes and Effects Analysis (FMEA) or Fault Tree Analysis is the analysis of a model structured to identify the various elements that can cause system failure by themselves, or in combination with others, based on the logic of the system. Fault tree analysis is typically used in engineering contexts. It can be adapted for use to identify risks by analyzing how risk impacts might arise. Another result is the probability of failure (or of reliability, mean time between failure, etc.) of the overall system, indicating the level of quality of the system or product. If the level of reliability is not acceptable, the Fault Tree can indicate where the system can be made more reliable—therefore, it is useful in the design and engineering phase of the project. An example is shown below.

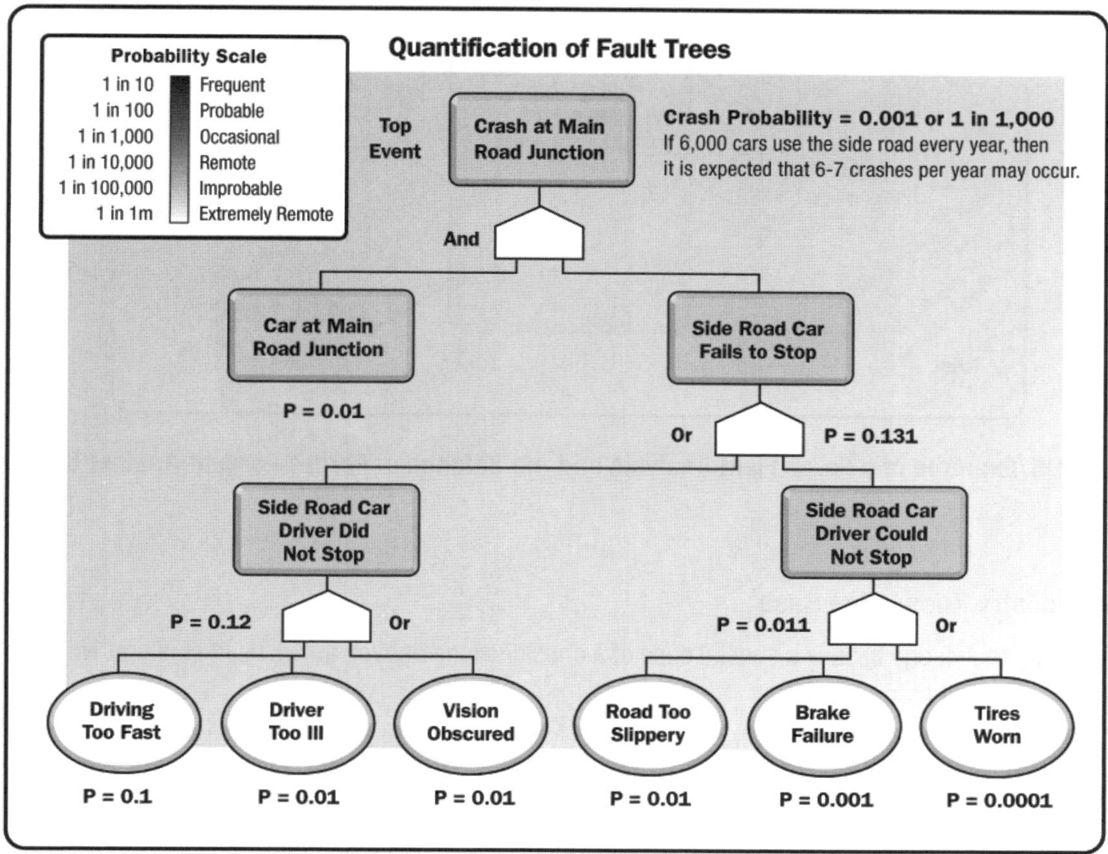

Figure D4. Fault Tree Analysis of the Possible Causes of a Crash at the Main Road Junction (this will be changed to be more project-oriented)

D.2.1.8 Force Field Analysis

Force Field Analysis is typically used in the change management context. It can be adapted for risk identification by identifying driving forces ("forces for change") and restraining forces ("forces against change") which currently affect achievement of a project objective. Risks can then be identified as uncertain events or conditions which would lead to a change in the strength of one or more of the identified forces. An example force field diagram is shown below.

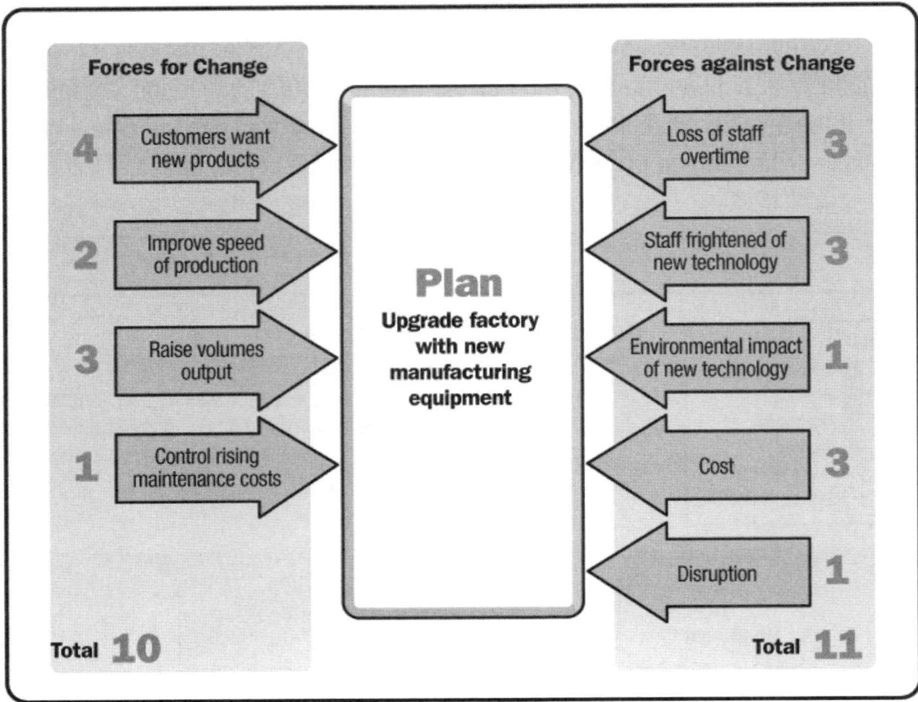

Figure D5. Example of a Force Field Analysis and the Balance of Forces For and Against Change

D.2.1.9 Industry Knowledge Base

An industry knowledge base is a special case of a checklist (see above), and is used similarly. No templates or examples are presented.

D.2.1.10 Influence Diagrams

An influence diagram is a diagrammatic representation of a project situation, showing the main entities, decision points, uncertainties, and outcomes, and indicating the relationships (influences) between them. The influence diagram can identify risks when combined with sensitivity analysis or Monte Carlo simulation to reveal sources of risk within the project. An example is shown below.

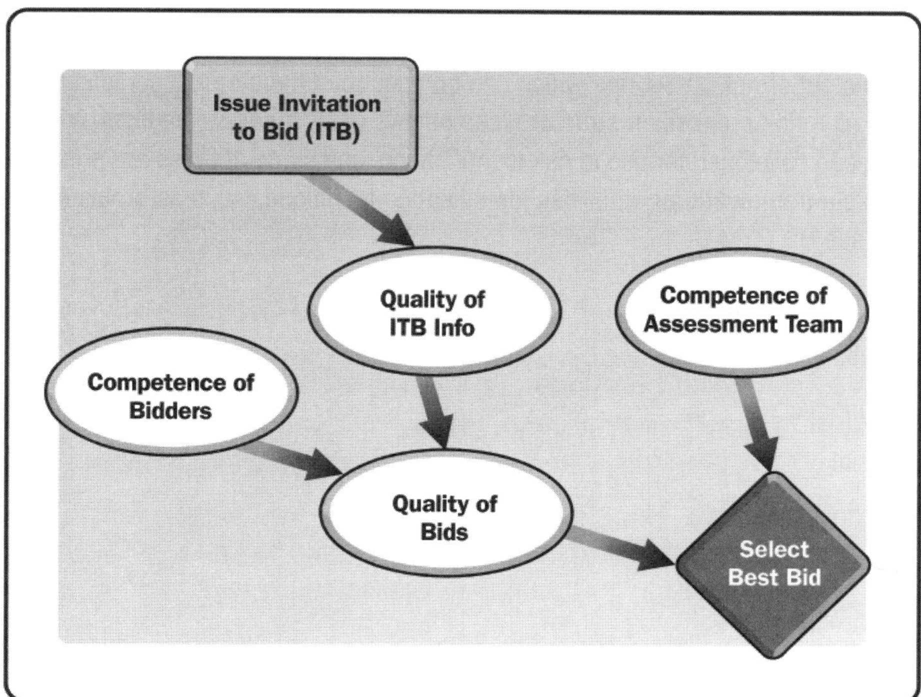

Figure D6. Example of an Influence Diagram in a Bidding Situation

D.2.1.11 Interviews

Risk identification interviews should include all main stakeholders and be conducted by an independent skilled interviewer using a structured agenda, in an atmosphere of confidentiality, honesty, and mutual trust. A risk breakdown structure, checklist or prompt list can be used as a framework for risk interviews. No templates or examples are presented.

D.2.1.12 Nominal Group Technique

The Nominal Group Technique is an adaptation of brainstorming where participants share and discuss all issues before evaluation, with each participant participating equally in evaluation. No templates or examples are presented.

D.2.1.13 Post-Project Reviews/Lessons Learned/Historical Information

Information relevant to risks for a current project can be obtained by reviewing databases of risks which occurred in previous similar situations. Such databases might arise from post-project reviews or lessons learned exercises. They may also exist as repositories of historical information, either within an organization or industry body. No templates or examples are presented.

D.2.1.14 Prompt Lists

A prompt list is a set of risk categories which can be used to stimulate risk identification. The prompt list may be presented as a risk breakdown structure (see below), or as a set of headings. A number of standard prompt lists have been developed for use in risk identification, and some of these are presented below. These can then be used as a framework for other risk identification techniques such as brainstorming (see D.2.1.2) or risk interviews (see D2.1.11).

1. The PESTLE prompt list:
    - Political
    - Economic
    - Social
    - Technological
    - Legal
    - Environmental
2. The TECOP prompt list:
    - Technical
    - Environmental
    - Commercial
    - Operational
    - Political
3. The SPECTRUM prompt list:
    - Socio-cultural
    - Political
    - Economic
    - Competitive
    - Technology
    - Regulatory/legal
    - Uncertainty/risk
    - Market

D.2.1.15 Questionnaire

A risk identification questionnaire can be presented as a special form of checklist (see D.2.1.4), where possible risks are shown in question format (for example "Is the client's requirement clearly defined?") rather than as risk statements ("The client may change the requirement after project start."). Alternatively a risk identification questionnaire can be used to present the headings from a prompt list (see D.2.1.14), asking questions such as "Are there any uncertainties arising from the use of technology on this project?" No templates or examples are presented.

D.2.1.16 Risk Breakdown Structure (RBS)

The risk breakdown structure (RBS) is a hierarchical framework of potential sources of risk to a project. An organization may develop a generic RBS for use across all its projects, or a project may use a project-specific RBS. A partial example RBS is shown below.

RBS LEVEL 0	RBS LEVEL 1	RBS LEVEL 2
ALL SOURCES OF PROJECT RISK	1. TECHNICAL RISK	1.1 Scope definition
		1.2 Requirements definition
		1.3 Estimates, assumptions, and constraints
		1.4 Technical processes
		1.5 Technology
		1.6 Technical interfaces
		Etc.
	2. MANAGEMENT RISK	2.1 Project management
		2.2 Program/portfolio management
		2.3 Operations management
		2.4 Organization
		2.5 Resourcing
		2.6 Communication
		Etc.
	3. COMMERCIAL RISK	3.1 Contractual terms and conditions
		3.2 Internal procurement
		3.3 Suppliers and vendors
		3.4 Subcontracts
		3.5 Client/customer stability
		3.6 Partnerships and joint ventures
		Etc.
	4. EXTERNAL RISK	4.1 Legislation
		4.2 Exchange rates
		4.3 Site/facilities
		4.4 Environmental/weather
		4.5 Competition
		4.6 Regulatory
		Etc.

Figure D7. Example of a Generic Risk Breakdown Structure

D.2.1.17 Root-Cause Analysis

A root cause analysis seeks to identify basic causes of risks that may be visible symptoms of more fundamental forces. It may also identify common sources of several risks, leading to broad-reaching risk response strategies. Similarly, care needs to be taken when using this technique for risk identification to distinguish between risks (uncertain causes of the impact) and issues (certain causes of the impact). In the diagram shown below the risks that were initially identified included rework, extra cost, schedule slips, low team morale, customer mistrust and repeated audits. An examination of the identified risks lead to a common root cause, that later phases of the project were typically started before the earlier ones were sufficiently mature. This organization repeatedly ignored the proper phase entry prerequisites, hastening later project stages in order to speed up the project.

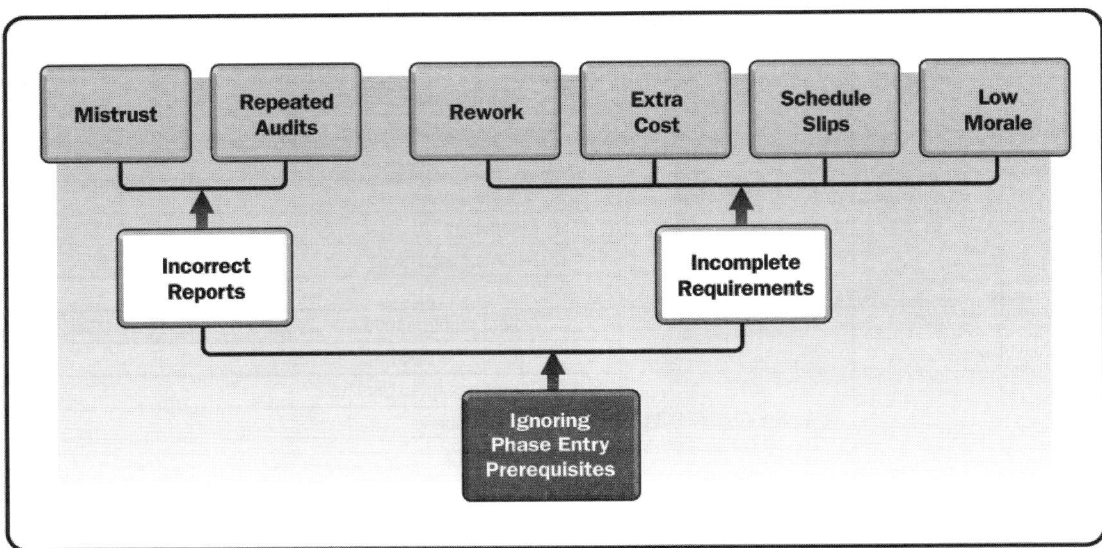

Figure D8. Example of a Root Cause Analysis

D.2.1.18 SWOT Analysis

SWOT Analysis identifies four characteristics of a given situation: strengths, weaknesses, opportunities and threats. The technique is commonly used in strategic decision making. It can be adapted for risk identification by changing the interpretation of the four perspectives, such that strengths and weaknesses relate to the characteristics of the organization conducting the project, and opportunities and threats identify the project risks. The technique is particularly useful for identifying internally-generated risks arising from within the organization. For example opportunities might be found by leveraging organizational strengths, or threats might arise as a result of organizational weaknesses, as illustrated below.

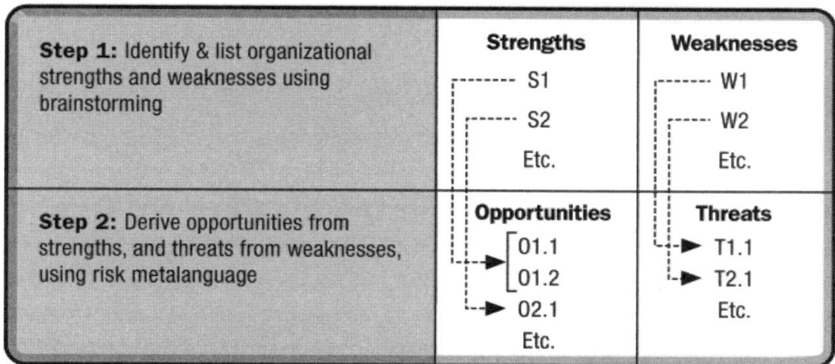

Figure D9. Example of a SWOT Analysis Structure

D.2.1.19 System Dynamics

System dynamics (SD) is a particular application of influence diagrams (see above), and can be used to identify risks within a project situation. The SD model represents entities and information flows within a project, and analysis of the model can reveal feed-back and feed-forward loops which lead to uncertainty or instability. In addition, the results of an SD analysis can show the impact of risk events on overall project results, such as the cost or schedule results to be expected. Analyses of changes in the model or assumptions can indicate the system's sensitivity to specific events, some of which may be risks. A simple example of an SD diagram is shown in Figure D11.

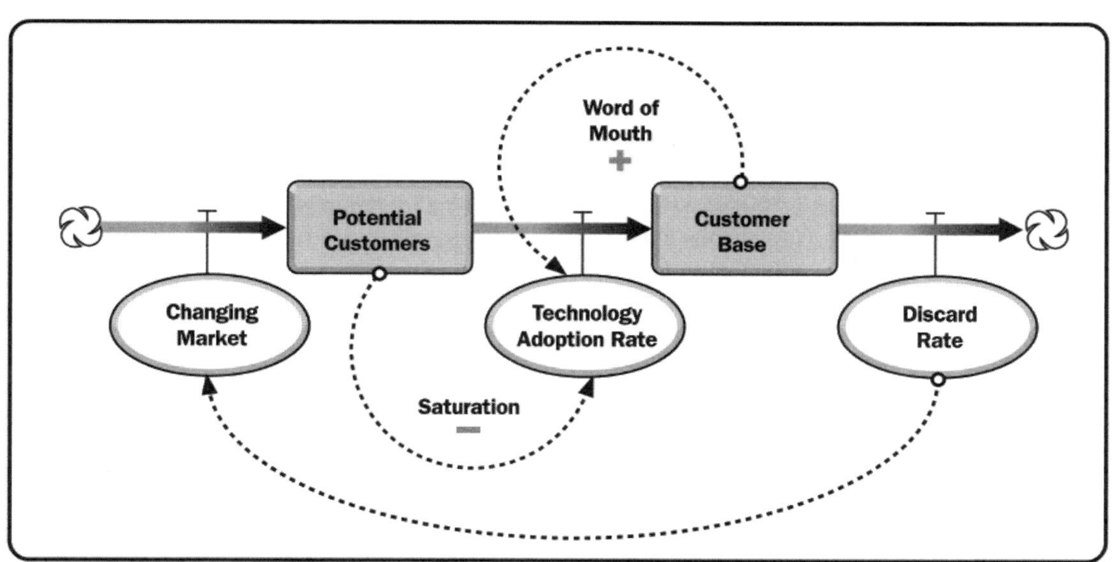

Figure D10. Example of a Simple System Dynamics Model with Feedback Loops

D.2.1.20 WBS Review

The work breakdown structure (WBS) for a project can form a framework for a number of other risk identification techniques, such as brainstorming, risk interviews, checklists or prompt lists. No templates or examples are presented.

D.3 Techniques, Examples and Templates for Perform Qualitative Risk Analysis (Chapter 6)

Perform Qualitative Risk Analysis prioritizes for further analysis or handling the undifferentiated list of risks that have been identified in the Identify Risks process. Organizations tend to apply resources to those designated as "high risk," based on their priority, often indicated by the risks' probability and impact characteristics.

D.3.1 Techniques for Perform Qualtitative Risk Analysis

Example of approaches are given in Table D3 and D.3.1.1 through D.3.1.3.

Table D3. Techniques for Perform Qualitative Risk Analysis

Technique	Strengths	Weaknesses	CSFs For Effective Application
Root Cause Analysis *See Chapter 5*			
Estimating techniques (applied to probability and impacts)	• Addresses both key dimensions of a risk, namely its degree of uncertainty (expressed as probability) and its effect on project objectives (expressed as impact)	• Difficult to calibrate if there is no historical database of similar events • Terms for probability (e.g. probable, almost certain) and for impact (e.g. insignificant, major) are ambiguous and subjective • Impacts can be uncertain or represented by a range of values that cannot be put into a specific impact level such as "moderate impact on time"	• Agreed definitions of probability and impacts which reflect stakeholders' risk tolerances and thresholds • Values used in the definitions represent the same level of impact across objectives as perceived by the organization's management or project stakeholders • Consistent use of these definitions across all identified risks

Table D3. Techniques for Perform Qualitative Risk Analysis *(continued)*

Technique	Strengths	Weaknesses	CSFs for Effective Application
			• Access to SMEs who have experience with the type of risk
Post-project reviews/ Lessons Learned/ Historical Information → *see Chapter 5*			
Probability and Impact Matrix (P-I Matrix)	• Allows the organization to prioritize the project risks for further analysis (e.g., quantitative) or risk response • Reflects the organization's level of risk tolerance	• Does not explicitly handle other factors such as urgency or manageability that may partly determine a risk's ranking. • The range of uncertainty in the assessment of a risk's probability or impact may overlap a boundary	• P×I matrix requires that the input data are clear and unambiguous in assigning levels of probability and impact • Effective estimation of impact and likelihood as outlined previously • Organizations should be careful to assess the combinations of probability and impact that qualify a risk as low, moderate or high risk so that the method used reflects the organization's risk attitude • Definitions used to designate the levels of impact (L, M, H) for each objective should represent the same level of impact as perceived by the organization's management or project stakeholders as reflecting the organization's utility function

(continued)

Table D3. Techniques for Perform Qualitative Risk Analysis *(continued)*

Technique	Strengths	Weaknesses	CSFs for Effective Application
Analytic Hierarchy Process	• Assists in developing a relative weighting for project objectives that reflects the organization's priorities for time, cost, scope and quality for the project • Assists the creation of an overall project priority list of risks created from the risks' priority with respect to individual objectives	• Organizational decisions are often made by committees, and individuals may not agree on relative priority among objectives • Difficult to gather the information about pair-wise comparison of the objectives from high-level management	• Expert facilitator in the process • Agreement by management that it is useful to develop a consistent set of priorities among objectives • Use of proper method or available AHP software
Root-Cause Analysis → *see Chapter 5*			

D.3.1.1 Estimating Techniques Applied to Probability and Impact

The probability of a risk occurring can be specified in several different ways. One common way is to assign levels of risk probability by ranges of probability. One benefit of this approach is that the subject matter experts only need to assess a risk's probability within a range rather than as a specific value. An example, assuming that a 5×5 Probability and Impact Matrix is desired, is shown in Figure D11 where the probability ranges are more tightly defined at low levels of probability.

Examples of impact level definitions are very project-specific. The values used to specify the level of impact from very low to very high (if a 5×5 matrix is being used) should be:

- Higher impact, for threats or opportunities, as they move from very low to very high for a specific objective
- Levels are defined by the organization as causing the same amount of pain or gain to the project for each level across objectives
- If a risk's possible impact is uncertain and could be assigned to more than one level of impact (e.g. from moderate to high) the analyst may choose to assign the risk to the impact level that represents the expected or average impact. Alternatively, the risk may be flagged for extra analysis in order to reduce the range of uncertainty to fit within a single range.

An example of impact level definitions is shown in Figure D11. These definitions should be tailored or scaled by stakeholders to the specific project. The definitions, appropriately tailored to the project, can be used for opportunities and threats.

SCALE	PROBABILITY	± IMPACT ON PROJECT OBJECTIVES		
		TIME	COST	QUALITY
VHI	61-99%	>40 days	>$200K	Very significant impact on overall functionality
HI	41-60%	21-40 days	$101K-$200K	Significant impact on overall functionality
MED	21-40%	11-20 days	$51K-$100K	Some impact in key functional areas
LO	11-20%	6-10 days	$11K-$50K	Minor impact on overall functionality
VLO	1-10%	1-5 day	$1K-$10K	Minor impact on secondary functions
NIL	<1%	No change	No change	No change in functionality

Figure D11. Example of Definitions for Levels of Probability and Impact on Four Specific Objectives Used to Evaluate Individual Risks.

Note—Opportunities are to be treated as representing a positive saving in time or cost, or increased functionality. For threats, each impact scale is interpreted negatively, i.e. time delays, increased cost, or reduced functionality.

D.3.1.2 Probability and Impact Matrix

Organizations typically assess a risk's priority on an objective from the combination of probability of occurrence and impact on that project objective, using definitions such as those shown in Figure D11. Risks are then placed on a probability and impact (P-I) matrix, such as one shown below. This matrix includes both threats and opportunities.

Probability and Impact Risk Ranking											
Probability	Threats					Opportunities					Probability
VHI	L	M	M	H	H	H	H	M	M	L	VHI
HI	L	L	M	H	H	H	H	M	L	L	HI
MOD	L	L	M	H	H	H	H	M	L	L	MOD
LOW	L	L	L	M	H	H	M	L	L	L	LOW
VLOW	L	L	L	L	M	M	L	L	L	L	VLOW
	VLOW	LOW	MOD	HI	VHI	VHI	HI	MOD	LOW	VLOW	
	Impact (Threats)					Impact (Opportunities)					

Figure D12. Example of Probability-Impact Matrix Used to Sort Risks (Threats and Opportunities) into High Risk (H), Moderate Risk (M) and Low Risk (L) Classes

D.3.1.3 Analytic Hierarchy Process (AHP)

AHP is a method to calibrate preferences for achieving the different objectives of a project. Do they prefer to achieve time more than cost? Is quality more important than scope? What is the relative weighting of the project's objectives in terms of their priority to the stakeholders or to management? The results are weights (summing to 100%) that reflect the relative priority of each objective. This prioritization can be important in determining how trade-offs affecting different objectives (e.g., Should we reduce scope to finish on time?) will be decided. It can also be used to create an overall project risk priority list from risks that have been assessed on their implications for individual objectives. Specialized software implementing AHP is available. A spreadsheet implementation is shown below.

Preference Factors	
1	Equally Preferred
2	Mildly Preferred
3	Moderately Preferred
4	Greatly Preferred
5	Always Preferred

Input Matrix (Preference Factors)				
	Cost	Time	Scope	Quality
Cost	1.00	0.25	0.33	0.20
Time	4.00	1.00	1.00	0.25
Scope	3.00	1.00	1.00	0.25
Quality	5.00	4.00	4.00	1.00

Note: Preference Factors input into the Dark Gray Area. Principal Diagonal is 1.0 by definition.
Other cells calculated as 1 / preference factor for same objectives.

Calculated Factors (Preference Factor / Column Total)					Weighting Factors
	Cost	Time	Scope	Quality	Average of Row
Cost	0.08	0.04	0.05	0.12	0.1
Time	0.31	0.16	0.16	0.15	0.2
Scope	0.23	0.16	0.16	0.15	0.2
Quality	0.38	0.64	0.63	0.59	0.6
Sum	13.00	6.25	6.33	1.70	1.0

Figure D13. Example of Analytic Hierarchy Process Computations to Determine the Relative Weighting of Four Project Objectives

D.4 Techniques, Examples and Templates for Perform Quantitative Risk Analysis (Chapter 7)

Perform Quantitative Risk Analysis seeks to determine the overall risk to project objectives when all risks potentially operate simultaneously on the project. It provides answers to several questions:

- How likely is the project to complete on the schedule date or earlier? How likely is the project actual cost to be the budgeted cost or less? How reliable will the product be that the project produces? What is the best decision to make in the face of uncertain results?
- How much contingency in time and cost is needed to provide the organization with its desired degree of confidence in the results? How should the design of the product or system be changed most economically to increase its reliability?
- What are the individual risks that seem to be the most important in determining the overall project risk?

D.4.1 Techniques for Perform Quantitative Risk Analysis

Examples of techniques for Perform Quantitative Risk Analysis are found shown in Table D4 and details are given in D.4.1.1 through D.4.1.5

Technique	Strengths	Weaknesses	CSFs For effective application
Decision Tree Analysis	• Causes the organization to structure the costs and benefits of decisions when the results are determined in part by uncertainty and risk • Solution of the decision tree helps select the decision that provides the highest Expected Monetary Value or expected utility to the organization	• It is sometimes difficult to create the decision structure • Probabilities of occurrences can be difficult to quantify in the absence of historical data • The best decision may change with relatively plausible changes in the input data, meaning that the answer may not be stable • The organization may not make decisions based on a linear Expected Monetary Value basis but rather on a non-linear utility function; utility functions are difficult to specify	• Careful structuring of the decision tree. All alternative decisions that are materially different should be considered; decision trees should be specified completely • Access to high-quality data about probability, cost and reward for the decisions and events specified using historical information or judgment of experts • Use of a utility function that has been validated with the organization's decision makers

(continued)

Technique	Strengths	Weaknesses	CSFs for Effective Application
		• The organization may not make decisions based on a linear Expected Monetary Value basis but rather on a non-linear utility function. Utility functions are difficult to specify • Decision tree analysis of complicated situations requires specialized (though available) software • There may be some resistance to using technical approaches to decision-making	• Availability and understanding of the specialized software needed to structure and solve the decision tree
Expected Monetary Value (EMV)	• EMV allows the user to calculate the weighted average (expected) value of an event that includes uncertain outcomes • It is well-suited to Decision Tree Analysis • EMV incorporates both the probability and impact of the uncertain events • EMV is a simple calculation that does not require specialized software	• Assessment of probability of risky events' occurring and of their impact can be difficult to make • EMV provides only the expected value of uncertain events; risk decisions often require more information than EMV can provide • EMV is sometimes used in situations where Monte Carlo simulation would be more appropriate and provide additional information about risk	• Identification of all possible events that need to be included in the EMV calculation • Access to historical data or expert opinions on the values of probability and impact that are needed for the calculation of EMV • Understanding of the difference between EMV and the output of simulation tools such as Monte Carlo analysis
FMEA/Fault Tree Analysis → *see Chapter 5*			

Technique	Strengths	Weaknesses	CSFs For Effective Application
Monte Carlo Simulation	• Used primarily for project schedule and cost risk analysis in strategic decisions • Allows all specified risks to vary simultaneously • Calculates quantitative estimates of overall project risk; reflects the reality that several risks may occur together on the project • Provides answers to questions such as (1) How likely is the base plan to be successful? (2) How much contingency in time and cost do we need to achieve our desired level of confidence? (3) Which activities are important in determining the overall project risk?	• Schedules are not simple and often cannot be used in simulation without significant de-bugging by an expert scheduler • The quality of the input data depends heavily on the expert judgment and the effort and expertise of the risk analyst • Simulation is sometimes resisted by management as being unnecessary or too sophisticated compared to traditional project management tools • Monte Carlo simulation requires specialized software which must be acquired and learned, causing a barrier to its use • Will produce unrealistic results unless input data include both threats and opportunities	• Creation of a good project model. Typical models include the cost estimate and the schedule • Use summary-level models such as project schedules and cost estimates • Access to high-quality data on risks including the risk's impact on project elements, uncertain activity durations and uncertain cost elements; the credibility depends on the quality of the data collected • Use of correct simulation tools
Post-project reviews/ Lessons Learned/ Historical Information → *see Chapter 5*			
System Dynamics → *see Chapter 5*			

D.4.1.1 Decision Tree Analysis

Decision tree analysis is usually performed using specialized, but widely available software. The software allows the user to specify the structure of the decision with decision nodes, chance nodes, costs, benefits, and probabilities. The user can also evaluate the different decisions using linear utility functions based on Expected Monetary Value or on non-linear utility functions of various shapes. An example is shown below where:

- The negative numbers represent outflows or investments (e.g. COTS)
- The percentages represent probabilities of the event occurring (e.g., Major Problems)
- The positive numbers represent rewards or values (e.g., after "Fix the Problem")
- "True" indicates the decision option taken from the square decision node, whereas "false" indicates the decision option not taken

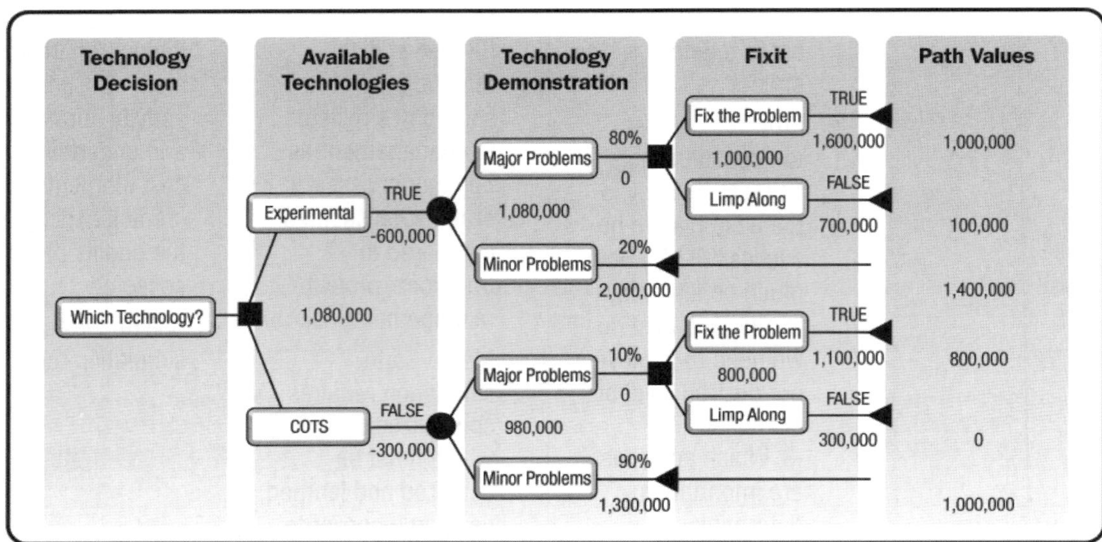

Figure D14. Example of a Decision Tree for Choosing between an Experimental Technology vs. Commercial Off the Shelf (COTS) Technology

Source: Precision Tree from Palisade Corporation

D.4.1.2 Expected Monetary Value

Expected Monetary Value (EMV) is a simple calculation of a value such as weighted average or expected cost or benefit when the outcomes are uncertain. All reasonable alternative outcomes are identified. Their probabilities of occurring (summing to 100%) and their values are estimated. The EMV calculation is made for the entire event by weighting the individual possible outcomes by their probabilities of occurring, as shown in Figure D15.

D.4.1.3 Monte Carlo Simulation

Monte Carlo simulation is a detailed, computer-intensive simulation approach to determining the value and probability of possible outcomes of a project objective such as a project schedule (e.g., the completion date) or cost estimate (e.g., the total cost). It computes the schedule or cost estimate many times using inputs drawn at

Example of an Expected Monetary Value (EMV) Calculation for a Business Strategy that Depends on Uncertain Market Demand			
Uncertain Outcome	**Reward ($000)**	**Probability (%)**	**Contribution to EMV**
High Market Demand	800	30%	240.0
Moderate Market Demand	450	45%	202.5
Low Market Demand	250	25%	62.5
TOTAL EMV			**505.0**

Figure D15. Example of an Expected Monetary Value Calculation when there are Three Uncertain Product Demand Scenarios

random from ranges specified with probability distribution functions for schedule activity durations or cost line-items. The solutions using these different input values are used to build a histogram of possible project outcomes and their relative probability, and cumulative probability from which to compute desired contingency reserves of time or cost. Additional results include the relative importance of each input in determining the overall project cost and schedule. Examples of the output of schedule and cost risk results are shown in Figures D16 and D17.

D.4.1.4 Monte Carlo Analysis of Finish Dates in Quantitative Schedule Risk Analysis

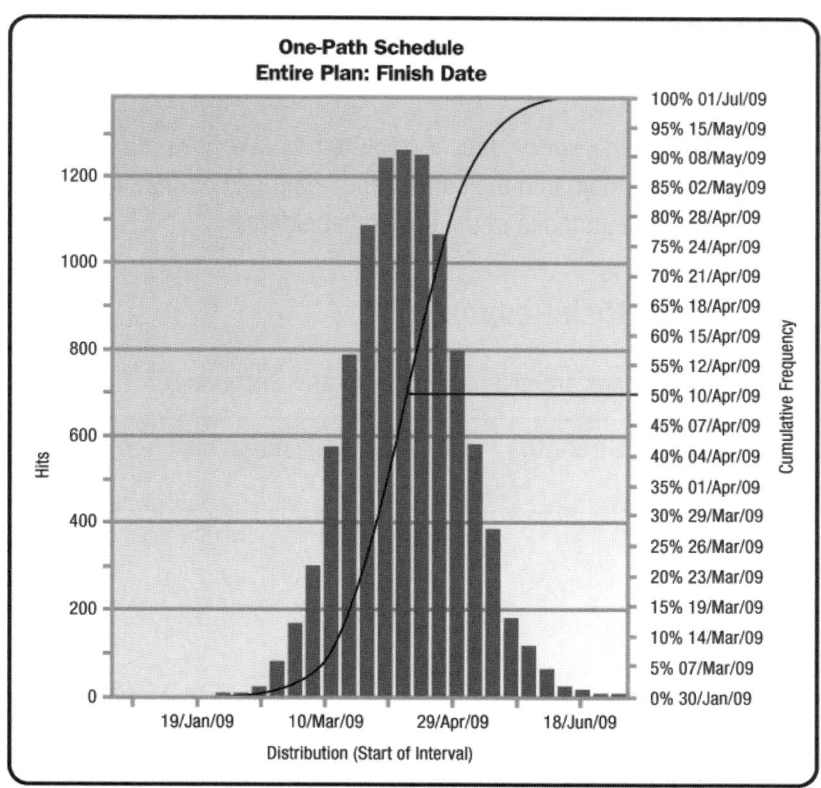

Figure D16. Example Histogram from Monte Carlo Simulation of a Project Schedule

Source: Pertmaster v. 8.0 Primavera Pertmaster

D.4.1.5 Monte Carlo Analysis of Project Cost at Completion in Quantitative Cost Risk Analysis

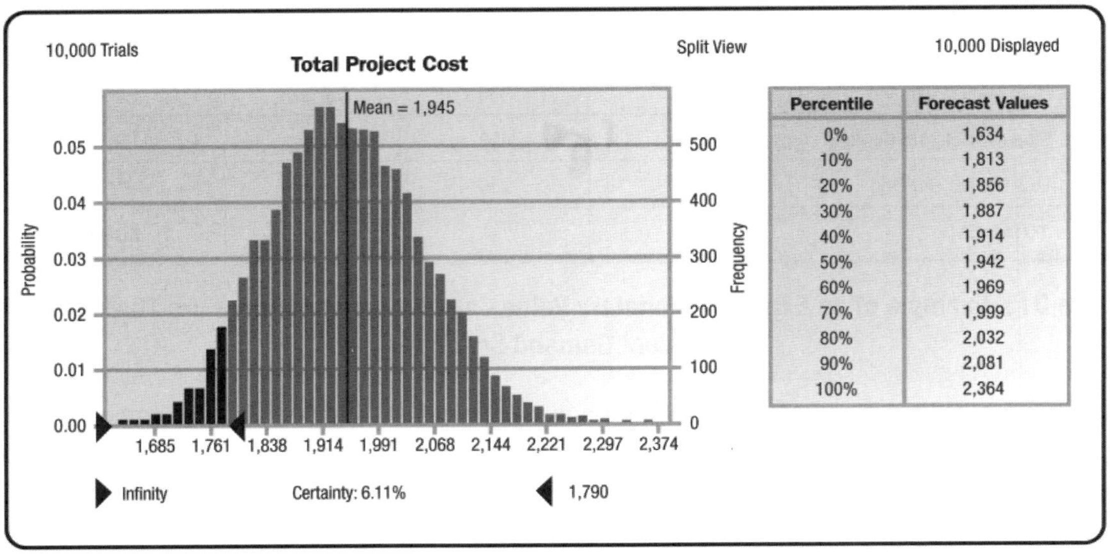
10,000 Trials
Total Project Cost
Split View
10,000 Displayed
Mean = 1,945
Probability
Frequency
0.05
0.04
0.03
0.02
0.01
0.00
500
400
300
200
100
0
1,685 1,761 1,838 1,914 1,991 2,068 2,144 2,221 2,297 2,374
Infinity
Certainty: 6.11%
1,790
Percentile | Forecast Values
0% 1,634
10% 1,813
20% 1,856
30% 1,887
40% 1,914
50% 1,942
60% 1,969
70% 1,999
80% 2,032
90% 2,081
100% 2,364

Figure D17. Example Histogram from Monte Carlo Simulation of a Project Cost Estimate
Source: Crystal Ball v. 7.3.8 from Oracle Hyperion (Decisioneering)

D.5 Techniques, Examples, and Templates for Plan Risk Responses (Chapter 8)

Plan Risk Responses develops the set of actions required to take into account the project's risks and their characteristics, and integrates them into the corresponding project management plan. The resultant plan should satisfy the risk appetites and attitudes of the key stakeholders.

D.5.1 Techniques for Plan Risk Response

Techniques for Plan Risk Responses are given in Table D5 and Sections D.5.1.1 through D.5.1.5.

Technique	Strengths	Weaknesses	CSFS for Effective Application
Brainstorming → *see Chapter 5*			
Check Lists → *see Chapter 5*			
Contingency planning	• Ensures that actions are available to address significant events before their occurrence	• Can give a false feeling of confidence – as if the risk had been avoided	• The trigger conditions must be clearly defined and tracked

Technique	Strengths	Weaknesses	CSFs for Effective Application
	• Allows rapid and focussed response • Improves image of professionalism of the way in which the project is managed		• The plans need to be validated periodically • Willingness of the organization to execute the plan and provide the budget and resources when the trigger condition occurs
Contingency reserve estimation	• Provides a rationale for reserves • Basis for constructive discussion with sponsor	• Makes the reserve visible and therefore liable to be reduced arbitrarily	• Policy for reserve management agreed with sponsor and senior management
Critical Chain Project Management (CCPM)	• Along with many other approaches, insists on resolving resource availability issues when developing the schedule • Addresses schedule risk by the addition of "feeding buffers" to absorb statistical variations on the durations of non-critical path activities to reduce their contribution to schedule risk • Partly mitigates financial risk by controlling the amount of "work in process" • "Buffer penetration" thresholds can be used as trigger condition for specific response actions • Special software is available for creating and managing the buffers	• Feeding buffers can deal with predictable common cause variation, but may be inadequate to cater for special causes • "Indicative" start and end dates can disturb conventional management expectations, and may cause problems for setting intermediate milestones • Assumption that base estimates represent 50% confidence levels (this weakness is not followed in all variants of this class of tool) • Not all project schedules are fully resourced	• Requires a fully resourced project schedule • Understanding of, and acceptance by management and project team members that the activity dates are indicative rather than definitive promises, being generally set to provide a 50% confidence level • Equitable sharing of the buffers by all team members concerned

(continued)

Technique	Strengths	Weaknesses	CSFs for Effective Application
Decision Tree Analysis → *see Chapter 7*	• Allows calculation of the expected monetary values of various response options as well as the value of the outcomes in the worst case and the best case		
Delphi Technique → *see Chapter 5*	• Involves selected experts in the process		
Expected Monetary Value (EMV) → *see Chapter 7*	• Provides an estimate of the potential benefit of a risk response		
Force Field Analysis → *see Chapter 5*	• The diagram can suggest where best to apply the responses		
Industry knowledge base → *see Chapter 5*	• Some risks have standard responses		
Interviews → *see Chapter 5*	• Experienced practitioners can provide both new ideas and act as "devil's advocate" for potential responses		
Nominal Group Technique → *see Chapter 5*	• Useful as a creativity technique for generating novel responses		
Multi-criterion selection techniques	• Provide a means of selecting the responses that best supports the full set of project objectives	• Can give counter-intuitive results	• Needs an agreed set of weighted project success criteria
Post-project reviews/ Lessons Learned/ Historical Information → *see Chapter 5*	• Leverages previous experience		

Technique	Strengths	Weaknesses	CSFs for Effective Application
Prompt Lists → *see Chapter 5*	• Stimulates creativity		
Quantitative Risk Analysis → *see Chapter 7*	• Provides a means of evaluating the potential effect of the response plans on the overall project risk	• Can be too involved or complex for the benefit envisaged	• Prior effective qualitative analysis
Root-Cause Analysis → *see Chapter 5*	• Allows the organization to identify and to address the fundamental causes of risks for efficient and effective responses; responding at the level of the root cause may effectively address multiple risks • Can provide a means of identifying symptoms for use as trigger conditions for contingent responses		
Scenario Analysis	• Provides view of the potential effect of the relevant risk and the corresponding response strategy • Forces the participants to analyze the effect of any strategy • Helps to identify secondary risks	• Adds to the list of assumptions • Can be time consuming	• All participants need a good understanding of the project plans

D.5.1.1 Contingency Planning

For specific (normally high-impact) risks, the risk owner may choose to assemble a team to develop a response, as if the risk had genuinely happened. The corresponding plan, with the supporting information, should then be documented and approved at project management or sponsor level. This approval must include authorization to deploy the corresponding resources if the predefined trigger conditions arise. No templates or examples are presented.

D.5.1.2 Contingency Reserve Estimation

All of the conditional response plans, as well any of the residual risks will, if they occur, have an effect on the schedule and/or budget and/or performance objectives of the project. An amount (time and cost) needs to be set aside to allow for these eventualities. This amount is made up of two components: those to cover specific, approved conditional responses (e.g. contingency plans), and those to address unspecified or passively accepted risks. Quantitative methods (see chapter 7) can be used to determine the amounts that should be set aside (e.g. decision trees for conditional responses, simulation for the set of unspecified risks). These reserves are tracked and managed in Monitor and Control Risks (chapter 9). No templates or examples are presented.

D.5.1.3 Multi-Criteria Selection Techniques

This is an adaptation of the Perform Qualitative Risk Analysis Process (chapter 6) based on selection criteria. The example below shows the use of a spreadsheet to calculate the weighted scores of two options, based on a predefined set of prioritized criteria: "points" is the product of "weight" by "rating."

Criterion	Weight	Option A		Option B	
		Rating	Points	Rating	Points
Price	9	8	72	10	90
Functionality	9	5	45	8	72
Ease of use	6	9	54	7	42
Lead time	7	9	63	6	42
Scores			**234**		**246**

Figure D18. Example of Comparing Options by their Ratings Along Four Prioritized Criteria

D.5.1.4 Scenario Analysis

Scenario analysis for risk response planning involves defining several plausible alternative scenarios (e.g. no change and all goes to plan, disaster occurs, utopia etc). The different scenarios may require different risk responses that can be described and evaluated for their cost and effectiveness. If the organization can choose between scenarios, the alternatives including the responses can be compared. If the scenarios are out of the control of the organization, the scenario analysis can lead to effective and necessary contingency planning.

No template is offered for this technique.

D.5.1.5 Critical Chain Project Management

A simple critical chain network is shown in Figure D19.

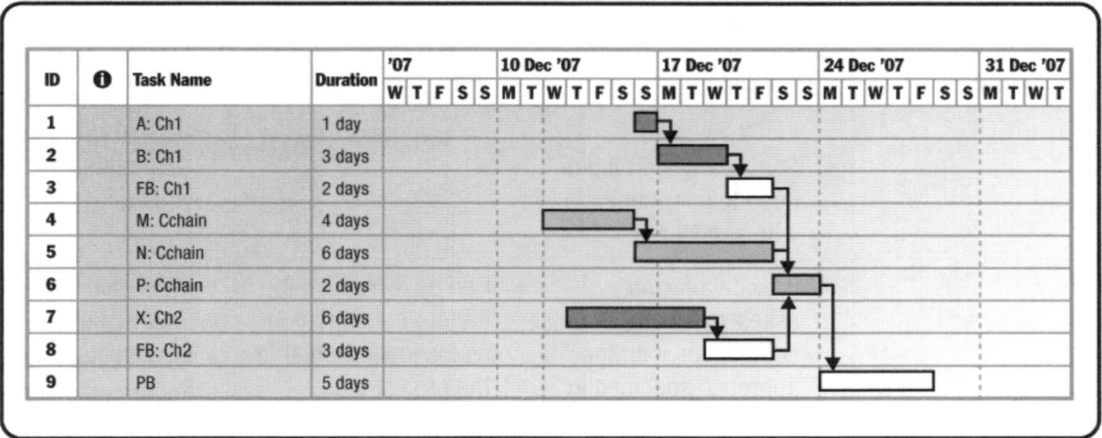

Figure D19. Simple Critical Chain Network

D.6 Techniques, Examples and Templates for Monitor and Control Risks (Chapter 9)

Monitor and Control Risks provides the assurance that risk responses are being applied, verifies whether they are effective and as necessary initiates corrective actions.

D.6.1 Techniques for Monitor and Control Risks Process

Techniques for Monitor and Control Risks are given in Table D6 and D.6.1.1 through D.6.1.6.

TABLE D6. Monitor and Control Risks Example

Technique	Strengths	Weaknesses	CSFs for Effective Application
Critical Chain Project Management (CCPM) → *see Chapter 8*	• Use of buffer penetration to trigger actions such as adjusting the relative priority of tasks		

(continued)

Technique	Strengths	Weaknesses	CSFs for Effective Application
Reserve Analysis	• Provides a means of tracking spend and releasing contingency amounts as risks expire; can be applied to schedule reserves in the same way • Gives early warning of need to communicate with sponsor	• Could lead to unwarranted focus on cost dimension • Attention to overall measure of reserve depletion may hide detailed risks	• Prior detailed reserve planning • Accurate sizing of the contingency reserve of time or cost relative to the risk to overall project completion date and budget
Risk Audits	• Provide a formal assessment of the compliance with the approach specified in the risk management plan	• Can be disruptive to the project and taken as too judgemental to the project team	• Well-specified risk management plan • Sensitivity to the burden it places on the project team
Risk Reassessment	• Forces a review of the project risks when it becomes necessary so that the risk register remains up-to-date	• Takes time and effort	• Well-maintained project and risk documentation scheme
Status Meetings	• Provide a means of verifying information about the status of risks (active, occurred, retired) and maintaining team understanding	• Can seem unnecessary to some participants	• Good meeting preparation and discipline
Trend Analysis	• Provides an indication of the effectiveness of earlier responses • Can provide trigger conditions for responses	• Requires understanding of significant vs. non-significant variation	• Regular reporting and analysis of the critical values

Technique	Strengths	Weaknesses	CSFs for Effective Application
Variance Analysis	• Allows comparison between forecast and actual risk impacts • Can provide trigger conditions for responses • Provides data for Earned Value Analysis which can be compared to quantitative risk analysis results	• Does not show relationship with earlier data • The values can be taken out of context	• Realistic prior definitions of thresholds for "significant variance"

D.6.1.1 Reserve Analysis

An analytical technique to determine the essential features and relationships of components in the project management plan to establish a reserve for the schedule duration, budget, estimated cost, or funds for a project. Tracking the state of the reserve through project execution will provide summary information as to the evolution of the status of the corresponding risks. This information can be useful when reporting up the organization to those responsible for several projects. In addition, once a corresponding risk occurs or ceases to be current (i.e. when it can no longer impact the project), the corresponding reserve needs to be reviewed in order to assess whether it still provides the agreed level of confidence.

Time buffers can be used in two different ways:

- To provide for accepted schedule risks, as described above or
- As a scheduling-related technique in critical chain project management (CCPM).

In contrast with the contingency reserve for identified risks, the buffers in CCPM provide a shared mechanism for accommodating the natural variability of activity durations over a sequence (or chain) of activities. Tracking the rate at which each such buffer is used during project execution provides valuable information at a given point in time as to the level of schedule risk along that chain, and is used in CCPM for adapting the priority or management focus for additional analysis and as necessary triggering further risk management activities.

No templates or examples are presented.

D.6.1.2 Risk Audits

Risk audits are carried out in order to evaluate:

- Are the risk management rules being carried out as specified?
- Are the risk management rules adequate for controlling the project?

No templates or examples are presented.

D.6.1.3 Risk Reassessment

The objective of risk reassessment is to ensure that the full risk management cycle is repeated as required to ensure effective control. See Figure D20.

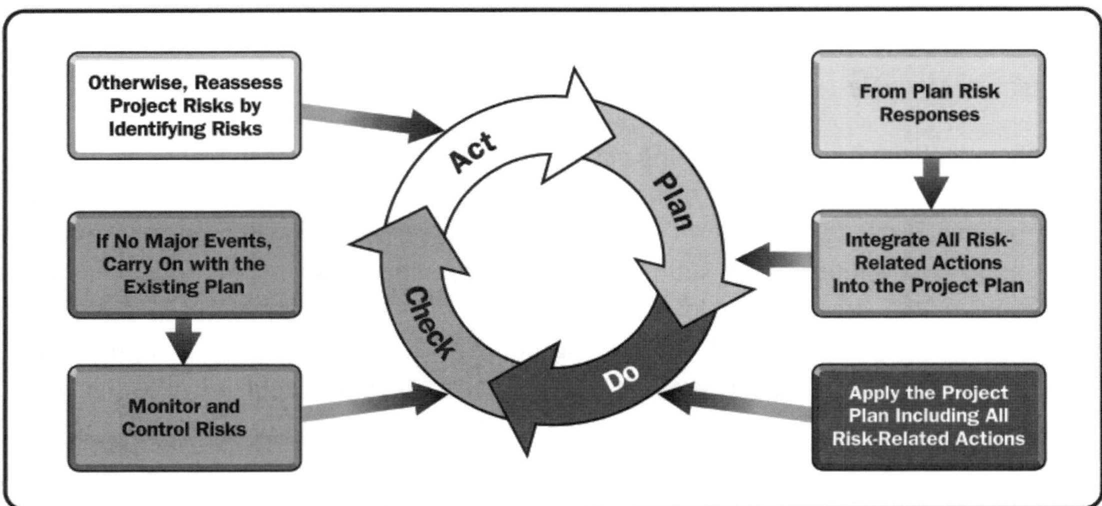

Figure D20. The Risk Reassessment Process

D.6.1.4 Status Meetings

Risks can and should be on the agenda at all project reviews. Typically, the agenda items should cover the following:

- Top priority risks at present.
    - Are there any changes?
- Risks or trigger conditions that have occurred.
    - What is the status of the actions?

- Risks responded to in the last period.
    - Effectiveness of actions taken.
    - Are there any additional actions required?
- Risks closed in the last period.
    - Impact on the plans.
- Lessons to be added to the Organizational Process Assets.

D.6.1.5 Trend Analysis

The evolution of the variance values over time should be analyzed in order to evaluate how the risk profile is changing, whether previous actions are having the expected effect and whether additional actions are required. The Earned Value formulae of the "to complete performance index" can be used to assess changes with respect to time and cost. No templates or examples are presented.

D.6.1.6 Variance Analysis

The formulae in Earned Value Analysis (CV, SV, CPI, SPI) can be used to set thresholds for action, and to indicate when the risk process may be ineffective. Earned value management systems (EVMS) use variance from plan as the basis of forecasts or extrapolations to the cost at completion. Projections made using EVMS have been shown by experience to be reliable early in the project, e.g., 20% into the execution. No templates or examples are presented.

APPENDIX E

REFERENCES

Association for Project Management. 2004. *Project risk analysis & management (PRAM) guide* (second edition). High Wycombe, Bucks UK: APM Publishing, ISBN 1-903494-12-5.

AS/NZS 4360:2004. Risk management. Published jointly by Standards Australia, Homebush NSW 2140, Australia, and Standards New Zealand, Wellington 6001, New Zealand, ISBN 0-7337-5904-1.

BS6079-3:2000. *Project Management—Part 3. Guide to the management of business-related project risk.* London, UK: British Standards Institute, ISBN 0-580-33122-9.

BS31100:2007 *Code of practice for risk management.* London, UK: British Standards Institute.

BS/IEC 62198:2001 *Project risk management—Application guidelines.* London, UK: British Standards Institute, ISBN 0-580-390195.

BSI/PD ISO/IEC Guide 73:2002. *Risk management vocabulary—Guidelines for use in standards.* London, UK: British Standards Institute, ISBN 0-580-401782.

IEEE Standard 1540-2001. *Standard for software life cycle processes—Risk management.* Piscataway, NJ, USA: Institute of Electrical and Electronic Engineers, Inc., 2001.

Institute of Risk Management (IRM), National Forum for Risk Management in the Public Sector (ALARM) and Association of Insurance and Risk Managers (AIRMIC). 2002. *A risk management standard.* London UK: IRM/ALARM/AIRMIC.

Institution of Civil Engineers, Faculty of Actuaries and Institute of Actuaries. 2005. *Risk Analysis & Management for Projects (RAMP) (second edition).* Westminster, London, UK: Thomas Telford, ISBN 0-7277-3390-7.

ISO 31000. *Risk management—Guidelines on principles and implementation of risk management.* Geneva, Switzerland: International Organization for Standardization.

JIS Q2001:2001(E). 2001. *Guidelines for development and implementation of risk management system.* Japanese Standards Association.

CAN/CSA-Q850-97. *Risk management: Guideline for decision-makers.* Ontario, Canada: Canadian Standards Association. ISSN 0317-5669.

Project Management Institute. 2004. *A guide to the project management body of knowledge (PMBOK® Guide)—* Third Edition. Newtown Square, PA USA: Project Management Institute.

UK Office of Government Commerce (OGC). 2007. *Management of risk—Guidance for practitioners.* London, UK: The Stationery Office, ISBN 0-11331038-2.

GLOSSARY

Assumptions. Assumptions are factors that, for planning purposes, are considered to be true, real, or certain without proof or demonstration. Assumptions affect all aspects of project planning and are part of the progressive elaboration of the project. Project teams frequently identify, document, and validate assumptions as part of their planning process. Assumptions generally involve a degree of risk.

Benefit. Positive effect on a project objective arising from the occurrence of an opportunity.

Bias. During information gathering about risk, the source of information exhibits a preference or an inclination that inhibits impartial judgment. Types of bias which commonly affect the risk process include cognitive and motivational bias.

Cause. Events or circumstances which currently exist and which might give rise to risks.

Consequence. See *impact.*

Constraint. The state, quality, or sense of being restricted to a given course of action or inaction. An applicable restriction or limitation, either internal or external to a project, which will affect the performance of the project or a process.

Contingency Reserve. The amount of funds, budget, or time needed above the estimate to reduce the risk of overruns of project objectives to a level acceptable to the organization.

Contingency Plan. A plan developed in anticipation of the occurrence of a risk, to be executed only if specific, predetermined trigger conditions arise.

Decision Tree Analysis. The decision tree is a diagram that describes a decision under consideration and the implications of choosing one or another of the available alternatives. It is used when some future scenarios or outcomes of actions are uncertain. It incorporates probabilities and the cost or rewards of each logical path of events and future decisions, and uses expected monetary value analysis to help the organization identify the relative values of alternative actions.

Effect. Conditional future events or conditions which would directly affect one or more project objectives if the associated risk happened.

Emergent Risk. A risk which arises later in a project and which could not have been identified earlier on.

Identify Risks. The process of determining which risks may affect the project and documenting their characteristics.

Impact. A measure of the effect of a risk on one or more objectives if it occurs. Also known as *consequence.*

Individual Risk. A specific uncertain event or condition which, if it occurs, has a positive or negative effect on at least one project objective.

Issue. See *problem.*

Likelihood. See *probability.*

Monitor and Control Risks. The process of implementing risk response plans, tracking identified risks, monitoring residual risks, identifying new risks, and evaluating the risk process throughout the project life cycle.

Monte Carlo Analysis. A technique that computes or iterates the project cost or project schedule many times using input values, selected at random from probability distributions of possible costs or durations, to calculate a distribution of possible total project cost or completion dates.

Objective. Something toward which work is to be directed, a strategic position to be attained or a purpose to be achieved, a result to be obtained, a product to be produced, or a service to be performed.

Opportunity. A condition or situation favorable to the project, a positive set of circumstances, a positive set of events, a risk that will have a positive impact on project objectives, or a possibility for positive changes. Contrast with *threat.*

Overall Project Risk. Overall project risk represents the effect of uncertainty on the project as a whole. Overall project risk is more than the sum of individual risks on a project, since it applies to the whole project rather than to individual elements or tasks. It represents the exposure of stakeholders to the implications of variations in project outcome measured in terms of the corresponding objectives.

Perform Qualitative Risk Analysis. The process of prioritizing risks for further analysis or action by assessing and combining their probability of occurrence and impact.

Perform Quantitative Risk Analysis. The process of numerically analyzing the effect of identified risks on overall project objectives.

Plan Risk Management. The process of defining how to conduct risk management activities for a project.

Plan Risk Responses. The process of developing options and actions to enhance opportunities and to reduce threats to project objectives.

Probability. A measure of how likely an individual risk is to occur. Also known as *likelihood.*

Problem. Negative effect on a project objective arising from occurrence of a threat.

Project Risk Management. Project Risk Management includes the processes concerned with conducting risk management planning, identification, analysis, responses, and monitoring and control on a project. The purpose of Project Risk Management is to increase the probability and impact of positive events and decrease the probability and impact of events adverse to project objectives.

Response Strategy. A high-level approach to address an individual risk or overall project risk, broken down into a set of risk actions.

Risk. An uncertain event or condition that, if it occurs, has a positive or negative effect on a project's objectives.

Risk Action. A detailed task which implements in whole or in part a response strategy in order to address an individual risk or overall project risk.

Risk Action Owner. The person responsible for carrying out the approved risk actions for responding to a given risk. Also known as "response owner" when the context allows it.

Risk Attitude. A chosen mental disposition towards uncertainty, adopted explicitly or implicitly by individuals and groups, driven by perception, and evidenced by observable behavior. Risk attitude exists on a continuous spectrum, but common risk attitudes include risk averse, risk tolerant, risk neutral and risk seeking.

Risk Breakdown Structure (RBS) [Tool] A hierarchically organized depiction of the identified project risks arranged by risk category and subcategory that identifies the various areas and causes of potential risks. The risk breakdown structure is often tailored to specific project types.

Risk Category. A group of potential causes of risk. Risk causes may be grouped into categories such as technical, external, organizational, environmental, or project management. A category may include subcategories such as technical maturity, weather, or aggressive estimating. See also *Risk Breakdown Structure (RBS)*

Risk Exposure. A measure of overall project risk describing the overall effect of identified risks on objectives.

Risk Management Plan. The document describing how Project Risk Management will be structured and performed on the project. It is contained in or is a subsidiary plan of the project management plan. The risk management plan can be informal and broadly framed, or formal and highly detailed, based on the needs of the project. Information in the risk management plan varies by application area and project size. The risk management plan is different from the risk register that contains the list of project risks, the results of risk analysis, and the risk responses.

Risk Metalanguage. A structured description of a risk which separates cause, risk, and effect. A typical risk description using risk metalanguage might be in the form: "Because of <cause>, <risk> might occur, which would lead to <effect>."

Risk Model. A representation of the project including data about project elements and risks that can be analyzed by quantitative methods.

Risk Owner. The person responsible for ensuring that an appropriate response strategy is selected and implemented, and for determining suitable risk actions to implement the chosen strategy, with each risk action assigned to a single risk action owner.

Risk Register. The document containing the results of the qualitative risk analysis, quantitative risk analysis, and risk response planning. The risk register details all identified risks, including description, category, cause, probability of occurring, impact(s) on objectives, proposed responses, owners, and current status.

Risk Threshold. A measure of the level of risk exposure above which action must be taken to address risks proactively, and below which risks may be accepted.

Root Cause. An initiating cause that gives rise to a causal chain which may give rise to risks.

Secondary Risk. A risk that arises as a direct result of implementing a risk response.

Stakeholder. Person or organization (e.g., customer, sponsor, performing organization, or the public) that is actively involved in the project, or whose interests may be positively or negatively affected by execution or completion of the project. A stakeholder may also exert influence over the project and its deliverables.

Threat. A condition or situation unfavorable to the project, a negative set of circumstances, a negative set of events, a risk that will have a negative impact on a project objective if it occurs, or a possibility for negative changes. Contrast with *opportunity*.

Trigger Condition. Circumstance under which a risk strategy or risk action will be invoked.

INDEX

R

S

T

U